North Carolina's legal system of a separate legal code governing slaves and slave crimes. The author states that as the eighteenth century advanced, North Carolina became in one respect much like the rest of the colonial South. As the slave population increased, remarkably so after mid-century, Carolina whites developed an outlook and way of life that became ever-present factors in a slave society. The two-tiered system of criminal courts, one for freemen and one for slaves, is a reflection of this outlook.

Crime and Society in North Carolina is the first work of its kind to examine the colony's legal past, and it will be an invaluable reference for historians. This important study reflects and illuminates the ways in which an early colonial judicial system mirrored the society it sought to control.

DONNA J. SPINDEL is professor of history at Marshall University in Huntington, West Virginia.

D1060340

Donna J. Spindel

CRIME AND SOCIETY IN
NORTH CAROLINA, 1663–1776

LOUISIANA STATE UNIVERSITY PRESS

Baton Rouge and London

Copyright © 1989 by Louisiana State University Press
All rights reserved
Manufactured in the United States of America

First printing

98 97 96 95 94 93 92 91 90 89   5 4 3 2 1

Designer: Laura Roubique Gleason
Typeface: Sabon
Typesetter: Composing Room of Michigan
Printer: Thomson-Shore, Inc.
Binder: John H. Dekker & Sons, Inc.

Library of Congress Cataloging-in-Publication Data
Spindel, Donna.
    Crime and society in North Carolina, 1663–1776 / Donna J. Spindel.
      p. cm.
    Bibliography: p.
    Includes index.
    ISBN 0-8071-1467-7 (alk. paper)
    1. Criminal justice, Administration of—North Carolina—History.
   2. Criminal courts—North Carolina—History.   I. Title.
    KFN7962.S65   1989
    364'.9756—dc19   88-30346
                                                 CIP

The paper in this book meets the guidelines for permanence and durability of the
Committee on Production Guidelines for Book Longevity of the Council on Library
Resources. ∞

For Stuart

CONTENTS

PREFACE

This study actually began on the day I walked into the stacks of the North Carolina State Department of Archives and History and found shelf after shelf filled with gray boxes and leather-bound volumes of court records. I had gone there to work on a study of female crime, but the abundance of surviving material, most of it untouched, led me to think about trying something much bigger. Here was an opportunity to examine one colony's criminal justice practices over a long period of time. Here was a massive amount of data, almost ready-made for quantification, that could be analyzed with a good deal of precision. From the beginning, I set two goals for myself. First, I wanted to present evidence as effectively as possible from a record series that had rarely been the subject of scholarly inquiry. Second, I hoped to offer an interpretation of early North Carolina society based on what I found.

North Carolina had originally attracted my interest because in a number of ways it seemed out of step with other southern communities. Sandwiched between the aristocratic slave societies of South Carolina and Virginia, North Carolina was, throughout much of its early history, a province of poor to middle-class farmers. It never enjoyed the rich cultural or intellectual life of its neighbors, nor did it share in their economic progress. But during the eighteenth century, North Carolina became, in one respect, much like the rest of the colonial South. As the slave population increased, remarkably so after mid-century, North Carolina whites developed the outlook and the way of life that were ever-present factors in a slave society.

Given all the subtleties and contradictions of North Carolina, the

colony has not been an easy one to study. Until the publication of
A. Roger Ekirch's *"Poor Carolina"* (1981), histories of the colony, with
the exception of several excellent analytical articles on the Regulation,
were largely narrative. For all its considerable strengths, however,
Ekirch's work scants the female, black, and poorer segments of society.[1]
Another area of Carolina studies that is in need of closer scrutiny is legal
history. This has been a long-neglected field for all the southern colonies, and there is, as yet, no comprehensive work on North Carolina
legal institutions and practices.[2] I hope in this work to remedy some of
these omissions.

Since the 1970s, historians have shown an increasing interest in
studying early American crime. They were not then, in any sense, blaz-
ing new paths, for scholars had decades earlier produced a number of
works that are still useful today. Those older studies systematically set
forth the evidence, describing the courts, defining the law, and citing the
most common offenses.[3] Drawing on an impressive array of analytical
tools, current historians, such as Douglas Greenberg, Michael Hindus,
and Peter Hoffer, advance beyond the "listing format" used by their
predecessors and look at crime within the context of the social, political,
and economic environment.[4] Yet the debate continues on exactly how to
do this. English scholars, whose keen interest in early crime helped to
stimulate Americans' research, offered some possibilities. J. M. Beattie,
for example, studied the court records of early England, measured the
incidence of particular criminal prosecutions, and related these offenses

1. A. Roger Ekirch, *"Poor Carolina": Politics and Society in Colonial North Carolina,
1729–1776* (Chapel Hill, 1981). See Peter H. Wood, Review of Ekirch, *"Poor Carolina,"*
in *North Carolina Historical Review,* LIX (1982), 192–93, journal hereinafter cited as
NCHR; Jeffrey J. Crow, Review of Ekirch, *"Poor Carolina,"* in *Journal of American
History,* LXIX (1982), 429–30.

2. David J. Bodenhamer and James W. Ely, Jr. (eds.), *Ambivalent Legacy: A Legal
History of the South* (Jackson, 1984), vii.

3. See George L. Chumbley, *Colonial Justice in Virginia* (Richmond, 1938); Arthur P.
Scott, *Criminal Law in Colonial Virginia* (Chicago, 1930); Raphael Semmes, *Crime and
Punishment in Early Maryland* (Baltimore, 1938); and Harry B. Weiss and Grace M.
Weiss, *An Introduction to Crime and Punishment in Colonial New Jersey* (Trenton,
1960).

4. Douglas Greenberg, *Crime and Law Enforcement in the Colony of New York,
1691–1776* (Ithaca, 1974); Michael S. Hindus, *Prison and Plantation: Crime, Justice,
and Authority in Massachusetts and South Carolina, 1767–1878* (Chapel Hill, 1980);
Peter C. Hoffer and William B. Scott (eds.), *Criminal Proceedings in Colonial Virginia:
[Records of] Fines, Examination of Criminals, Trials of Slaves, etc., from March 1710
[1711] to [1754] [Richmond County, Virginia]* (Athens, Ga., 1984).

to population changes, economics, and war. Using a slightly different method, Douglas Hay argued that the ideology of the ruling class is reflected in the criminal law. Instead of searching the records for evidence of criminality, he looked for prosecution patterns and showed how they mirror the courts as tools of social control. American historians branch off in various directions. Cynthia Herrup offers valuable insights into early English perceptions of crime and criminal behavior. Starting from the seventeenth-century belief that all men and women are sinners, she suggests the importance of the community's role in distinguishing between human weakness and genuine evil. Bradley Chapin argues that seventeenth-century colonists made criminal justice practices more rational and humane, and Peter Hoffer describes the early Virginia courts as "agents of social control" that emphasized deference to authority. Greenberg offered a succinct comment on this variety of perspectives when he wrote that "those few of us who have been working in the field not only differ about which are the right answers, we do not even agree about which are the right questions."[5]

Lacking a consensus on the most appropriate way to interpret crime, I have tried in this book to develop a fairly simple methodology. Most definitions of crime, for example, are Blackstone's or those of other eighteenth-century legal writers. When looking for rates of resolution, I considered all cases that came before grand juries as well as petit juries. In determining rates of resolution for different offenses, or in relating gender or social status to crime, I used the cross-tabulation capacity of the computer. I also decided at the outset to analyze all surviving data, because if I had sampled the records of a county or region over time, I would not have been able to achieve the comprehensive analysis I sought.

I believe that the criminal court records give us a picture of early North Carolina that is, in important ways, different from previous ones. The records show, for example, that "poor" Carolina, apparently so

5. J. M. Beattie, "Crime and the Courts in Surrey, 1736–1753," in J. S. Cockburn (ed.), *Crime in England 1550–1800* (Princeton, 1977), 155–86; Douglas Hay, "Property, Authority and the Criminal Law," in Hay *et al.*, *Albion's Fatal Tree: Crime and Society in Eighteenth-Century England* (New York, 1975), 17–63; Cynthia B. Herrup, "Law and Morality in Seventeenth-Century England," *Past and Present*, CVI (1985), 102–23; Bradley Chapin, *Criminal Justice in Colonial America, 1606–1660* (Athens, Ga., 1983); Hoffer and Scott (eds.), *Criminal Proceedings in Colonial Virginia*, xxxi; Douglas Greenberg, "Crime, Law Enforcement, and Social Control in Colonial America," *American Journal of Legal History*, XXVI (1982), 316, journal hereinafter cited as *AJLH*.

backward, developed a comparatively sophisticated criminal court structure, fully capable of reproducing English practices as well as those of other colonies. Much has been made of the colony's fledgling elites contending for power and commanding little respect from an unruly populace. Yet the data portray a society that gave highest priority to order and stability. A lack of deference could not have weakened colonial institutions because evidence from the records gives every indication that deference prevailed. Threatened at times by political strife, the courts still served as a crucial core of stability, both representing and imposing order.

Criminal court data also bring to center stage a host of characters who, until now, have existed largely in the shadows of Carolina history. The poor and the powerless, white and black, male and female, now come forward to occupy a highly visible place. What was it like then to be propertyless, female, or black? Granted, crime data do not tell the whole story. But according to the evidence, certain assumptions about gender, status, and race filtered through a legal system that was, in fact, managed by elites. No systematic oppression of poor whites or women occurred, but perceptions of property and a woman's expected place in society had a discernible impact on judicial decision-making. When it came to blacks, the records make clear that this bottom quarter of the population could find no solace in the law. Brutal as it was, the law on black crime reflected slaves' oppressed condition in the society at large. And evidence from the criminal court records makes the significant presence of slaves in the colony all the more apparent.

The primary sources for this book are the records generated by the Carolina courts. This material represents virtually the only documentary evidence from the colony's early history and is an exceedingly important supplement to the surviving evidence from later years. But the court records are not infallible sources.[6] In fact, the Carolina data present two common problems: first, the absence of court records for various periods in different jurisdictions, due to fire, decay, or carelessness; and second, the questionable reliability of the records that do exist. For example, the higher court records series is interrupted by long,

---

6. See, for example, Michael G. Kammen, "Colonial Court Records and American History," *American Historical Review,* LXX (1965), 732–39; and Greenberg, "Crime, Law Enforcement, and Social Control," 293–325.

irregular gaps. Data for fourteen out of thirty-five county court jurisdictions are missing. Important documents cover the early years, but the bulk derives from the thirty-five-year period before the Revolution. Some of the surviving material, valuable as it is, is in poor condition, and many of the documents are marred by minor frustration-causing inconsistencies—variations in spelling, incorrect dating, and multiple socioeconomic labels. Yet these are problems that can be overcome. In the Note on Methods, I outline briefly how I have dealt with them. I did no sampling, for example, that might have produced skewed results, given the nature of the documents. Indeed, I believe my findings are strengthened by the fact that this is a comprehensive study. No available data are excluded.

ACKNOWLEDGMENTS

A number of people gave generously of their time to read the manuscript and share with me their expertise. No one was more helpful than Warren M. Billings, who responded to early drafts with both criticism and encouragement. Peter Wood also read the manuscript from beginning to end and helped me redirect my thinking and fill in the gaps. Others who read and commented on the manuscript at various stages of its development included William S. Price, Jr., Jeffrey Crow, and Robert Cain, all at the North Carolina Archives. Michael Kay sent me his then-unpublished studies of slave crime in North Carolina. My colleagues and friends at Marshall tolerated my single-minded research interests for a long time, and I benefited greatly from their perspectives on my work. For this, I thank David Duke, William Palmer, and Michael Galgano (now at James Madison University).

During the many months I spent at the Archives in Raleigh, the staff made me feel at home. Not only did they provide me with a comfortable place to work, but they also were unfailingly helpful. George Stevenson, Reference Unit Supervisor, shared his extensive knowledge of the legal records. Barbara Cain and Ellen McGrew always had the time to answer questions. I cannot imagine a better environment in which to conduct a long-term research project.

Grants from the American Philosophical Society gave me the time to collect the data for this study. Marshall University encouraged my research through financial support during the summer months, a sabbatical leave, and released time from teaching. The staff of the Computer Center went beyond the call of duty, generating thousands of cards for me and promptly returning my output. This kind of support is a great deal to receive from a university that has traditionally emphasized its teaching role. In my own department, Yvonne Tumblin and Sally Keaton spent many hours typing and correcting and retyping the manuscript. Unfailingly friendly, they never seemed perturbed about making a change "one more time."

On the personal side, I thank my parents, who instilled in me at a very early age a love of and appreciation for history. I thank Megan S. Thomas, who was not here on earth when I began this book and who, despite her best efforts to the contrary, still allowed me to finish it. Finally, I thank Stuart W. Thomas, Jr., Professor of Psychology at Marshall University, as fine a statistician (and husband) as can be found anywhere. For many more hours than I dare recount, he cheerfully took time from his own work to help me with mine. Time and again he lent his considerable expertise to the quantitative aspects of this project, steering it smoothly through the requirements of data preparation and programming. His help was the key that made this project work. He and I know well that in both a personal and professional way, this book would not have been possible without him.

NOTE ON METHODS

North Carolina criminal court records can be divided into dockets, minutes, and file papers. The Crown dockets provide the most basic information—the list of cases before a court session, the name of each defendant, a terse summary of the action in each case, the verdict, and, occasionally, the sentence. Very few dockets contain all categories of information. It is by no means unusual, for example, for a case to be continued from one docket to another until it disappears from the records altogether. Court minutes, if combined with dockets, can help fill in the missing parts of a case. These are the most plentiful of the documents, containing details about the date and location of the court session, the presiding and assistant justices, the grand and petit jury members, actions of the grand jury, formal indictments, pleas, verdicts, and sentences. A complete set of minutes, invaluable historical evidence, nevertheless falls short of providing all the information the historian would like to have. Indictments, for instance, are all recorded in standard legal form, which is much the same as the English model and thereby blurs the nuances that might distinguish one case from another. These documents are also silent about the events leading to a crime, how the accused was apprehended, the motives of the accused, etc. The file papers, a miscellaneous collection of materials, present the investigator with a tedious task. They consist of a multitude of loose papers, many of which have limited use, but some of which may be exceedingly important. Writs and recognizances form the bulk of the file papers, but occasionally case testimonies can be found slipped between the pages of other legal documents. The higher court records are available largely in published form through 1730 and in manuscript form for the duration of the colonial period. County court records have been published sporadically in local histories, but nearly all the original records are deposited, along with the higher court data, at the North Carolina Archives in Raleigh. All these records have been consulted for this study.

Since the court records contain literally thousands of cases, each one yielding various bits and pieces of information about the courts, the accused, and the alleged crimes, it seemed appropriate to use a computer to store, retrieve, and summarize the data. Thus the evidence could be prepared for analysis in a mere fraction of the time that more conventional means would take. This study makes use of simple programming—the FREQ procedure of the SAS statistical analysis system—and basic statistical techniques. There was no reason, for example, to use tests of statistical inference because there could be no sampling error; the entire known criminal defendant population was included in the analysis. Moreover, the application of sophisticated statistical analysis to data that are limited in amount and reliability runs the risk of producing deceptive results.[1]

Eighteen categories of information were selected as being most useful to achieve the goals of this study: name of the accused, sex, socioeconomic status, date of offense, location of offense, offense, date of trial, location of trial, court, plea, verdict, date of verdict, sentence, individual identification code, source, accuracy of source, case identification number, and indictment identification number. Every surviving court record was searched for these categories of information—few documents yielded all, and most just a few. Each category of information or variable was then coded for keypunching. This procedure generated a card for every action against a particular defendant. The computer was then programmed to accomplish a number of tasks: to summarize information for a single variable (how many men were in the defendant population?), to compare or cross-tabulate two variables (how many women were charged with assault?), and to cross-tabulate three variables (what sentences were imposed on men convicted of assault?). The tables in this study resulted from these analyses. Certain procedural problems inevitably arose. How, for example, were the accused to be identified as the

1. For an explanation of a similar approach, see Edward L. Ayers, *Vengeance and Justice: Crime and Punishment in the 19th-Century American South* (New York, 1984), 277.

same or different individuals when spelling was erratic or when the name John Bell or William Parker appeared time and again? In such cases, the site of the offense, the date, or the occupation of the accused could help establish identity. If no reasonable certainty could be achieved, the defendants in question were considered to be different individuals.[2]

In addition to the quantitative data gathered for this study, much non-quantifiable material was collected through regular note-taking. The published colonial records, which include the official papers of the colony, as well as a number of contemporary accounts proved useful in setting the background for, filling in the details of, and confirming the events described in the court records.

2. See Greenberg, *Crime and Law Enforcement in New York,* 209; and Kai T. Erikson, *Wayward Puritans: A Study in the Sociology of Deviance* (New York, 1966), 209–10.

CRIME AND SOCIETY IN NORTH CAROLINA

I

THE COLONIAL BACKGROUND TO CRIME
AND THE COURTS

[T]he people indeed are ignorant
—William Gordon

In the early 1660s a visitor to the northern section of the new Carolina colony would have found sandy beaches and pine forests in the east, gentle hills in the central area that became known as the Piedmont, and gradually, as the traveler went west, a mountainous region sliced by thousands of valleys. With the already established province of Virginia to the north and what would become, in 1712, the colony of South Carolina along the southern border, North Carolina offered settlers a mild climate and excellent land. Yet this promising venture proved that even with a great deal of planning and a bright future, something can still go wrong. Partly because of proprietary neglect and the resulting instability, the colony limped along until 1729 when its founders, having despaired of ever making the colony a paying proposition, sold out to the Crown. Once under royal control, North Carolina and its fortunes improved. By mid-century, through immigration and natural increase, the white population was growing quickly. While the majority of white males owned land, their holdings were typically small. Pockets of wealth could be found, particularly in the east, but no great planter aristocracy emerged. In one respect, however, the Carolina colony was beginning to mirror the rest of the South. By mid-century, slavery was a rapidly growing institution, one that would eventually comprise 25 percent of the total population. Thus the Carolina colony inevitably developed all the attitudes and outlooks that are so closely associated with a slave society.[1]

1. Among the best studies of the colony are Harry R. Merrens, *Colonial North Carolina in the Eighteenth Century: A Study in Historical Geography* (Chapel Hill, 1964); Hugh T. Lefler and William S. Powell, *Colonial North Carolina: A History* (New York,

Charles II granted the eight original Carolina proprietors a charter for a huge tract of New World territory in 1663.[2] They expressed their hopes and objectives in the charter, the Concessions and Agreements (1665), and in the Fundamental Constitutions (1669). Above all, Carolina was to be a money-making venture; but beyond the profit side, the proprietors planned to create their own feudalistic society governed by a colonial nobility. They made the Carolina province a palatinate, carved up into counties. They called the northern region Albemarle. Had the original plan succeeded, land would have been distributed to feudal lords and freeholders, thus ensuring them a dominant place in the colony's affairs. As it happened, the proprietors eventually turned to a more conventional means of government. In 1691, they appointed a deputy governor for the northern region. They also provided that a legislature of freeholders make laws in conjunction with the governor and that a liberal amount of religious freedom be permitted.

To bring their plan to fruition, the proprietors needed settlers. True, a number of Virginians had already established themselves in the Carolina region, but the proprietors also tried to attract settlers from Europe. They first launched a pamphlet campaign, describing the colony's most attractive features. Then they offered a limited period of freedom from debt prosecution (a law responsible, in part, for North Carolina's reputation as a gathering place for thieves), exemption from some taxes, and certain benefits in the Indian trade. They also encouraged slavery: "Every Freeman shall have absolute Authority over his Negro Slaves." By the turn of the century, the proprietors' efforts to develop their colony had failed to yield impressive results. Only a few thousand white settlers populated the area along with perhaps a thousand blacks. Scattered in the northeast, most free whites had come from Virginia. Moving south, they found a province with virtually no towns or villages and with no major trading area. Still, this seemingly secluded place, wracked by turmoil, experienced some growth. In 1696 a new county, Bath, was

---

1973); Ekirch, "*Poor Carolina*"; Jeffrey J. Crow, *The Black Experience in Revolutionary North Carolina* (Raleigh, 1977); and a series of articles by Michael Kay and Lorin Lee Cary. Excellent analyses can also be found in the introductory passages of each volume of Mattie Erma Edwards Parker, William S. Price, Jr., and Robert Cain (eds.), *North Carolina Higher-Court Records* (5 vols.; Raleigh, 1963–81), hereinafter cited as *NCHCR*.

2. On the early period of North Carolina history, see Lefler and Powell, *Colonial North Carolina*; *NCHCR*, I–IV; and William L. Saunders, Stephen B. Weeks, and Walter Clark (eds.), *The Colonial and State Records of North Carolina* (Raleigh, Winston, Goldsboro, and Charlotte, 1886–1914), I–IV, hereinafter cited as *NCSR*.

formed just south of Albemarle to accommodate the influx of settlers. A few years later a group of French Huguenots from Virginia occupied fertile land in the Pamlico River area, which, along with Albemarle Sound, shaped a peninsula that eventually became part of a new county called Granville. At this time the proprietors began a practice that paved the way for bitter sectional controversy. They allowed Albemarle County to hold a distinctly privileged position in government affairs: there were five assemblymen from each of its precincts, but the precincts of all other counties, as they were formed, would have two.[3]

Always interested in attracting newcomers, the proprietors welcomed, in the early 1700s, a most promising attempt at settlement. A group of Germans from the Rhine Palatinate and of Swiss from the town of Bern established their community between the Neuse and Cape Fear rivers, at a site they called New Bern. The settlers brought with them varied skills and plans to establish a center for trade. But after several years, their presence set off a bloody conflict with the Indians that nearly destroyed the colony and that led to the exclusion of whites from the fertile region for some time. Only much later did New Bern become a substantial settlement.

No further efforts at organized settlement helped to populate the colony during the proprietary period. When North Carolina became a royal province in 1729, the population consisted largely of English men and women; several thousand blacks; a few French, Germans, and Swiss; and probably a handful of Scotch-Irish. While the center of activity remained the northeast, attention was shifting southward, once again to the Cape Fear region. In the 1720s, under questionable authority, the governor had granted large pieces of Cape Fear property to favored colonists. Since the typical Carolina grant was relatively small, this short-lived period of substantial land grants established a unique configuration of landownership in this area of the colony. All the recipients of the governor's largesse—families such as Moore, Allen, Porter, Moseley, Swann, and Ashe—had moved from South Carolina with their slaves or from Albemarle. They all became active and prominent in provincial affairs and strove to make the Cape Fear a dominant region.

3. *NCHCR*, I, 150; Marvin L. Michael Kay and Lorin Lee Cary, "A Demographic Analysis of Colonial North Carolina with Special Emphasis Upon the Slave and Black Populations," in Jeffrey J. Crow and Flora J. Hatley (eds.), *Black Americans in North Carolina and the South* (Chapel Hill, 1984), 72; Lefler and Powell, *Colonial North Carolina*, 56.

By 1729, the eastern edge of North Carolina was occupied, but sparsely. The colony was still relatively underdeveloped, though the towns of Edenton to the north and New Bern to the south had become substantial settlements. They were also fast becoming bitter political rivals, particularly as the Cape Fear enjoyed steady growth. Drawing settlers from northern colonies, from other areas of North Carolina, and from Scotland, this area soon threatened Albemarle's favored position. Indeed, the royal period was a time of significant growth for the colony as a whole. Attracted by cheap and fertile land, immigrants helped North Carolina's population to rise quickly. In 1732, Governor George Burrington estimated the number of whites at 30,000, blacks at 6,000, and Indians at 800. By the 1750s, the white population had more than doubled; in the next decade, it nearly tripled to 124,000; and by the time of the Revolution, it had reached close to 200,000. As the white population expanded, settlement inevitably shifted west. Several thousand Scotch-Irish migrated to counties that bordered South Carolina. German immigrants, most from northern colonies, settled farther west. Through natural increase and immigration, the number of blacks increased even more rapidly than did the number of their white masters. By the 1750s, about 19,000 blacks populated the colony; on the eve of the Revolution, the number had risen to 52,000. Even though slaves probably did not compose more than one-quarter of the colonial population at any particular time, their concentration in the colony varied greatly. While blacks were a very small percentage of the population of the western counties, after mid-century they composed nearly 30 percent in some eastern counties and as much as 60 percent in the Lower Cape Fear. Historians Michael Kay and Lorin Lee Cary have noted a similarity between the way of life that evolved in the slave-dominated Chesapeake and in some of North Carolina's eastern counties.[4] Certainly by 1750, North Carolina was already experiencing the tensions, anxieties, and complex interrelationships inherent in a slave society.

North Carolina's white population is conventionally described as comfortably poor, living at a "near subsistence level," but still enjoying extensive landownership, which precluded extreme poverty. Even "the best estates in this country are but very moderate," noted Governor William Tryon in 1768. Such comments notwithstanding, it is well

4. George Burrington to Board of Trade, January 1, 1733, in *NCSR*, III, 433; Merrens, *Colonial North Carolina in the Eighteenth Century;* Kay and Cary, "A Demographic Analysis of Colonial North Carolina," in Crow and Hatley (eds.), *Black Americans.*

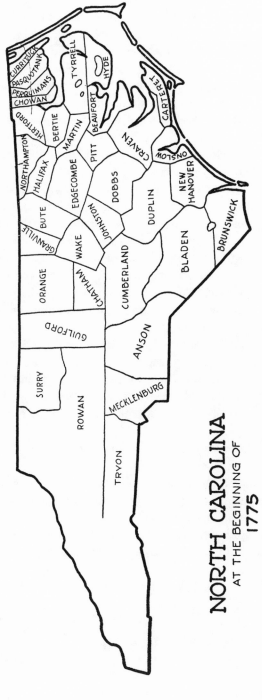

NORTH CAROLINA
AT THE BEGINNING OF
1775

Showing Approximate County Divisions
within Present State Boundaries

Map by
L. Polk Denmark.

From David L. Corbitt, *The Formation of the North Carolina Colonies, 1663–1943* (Raleigh, 1950). Reprinted by permission of the North Carolina Division of Archives and History.

worth noting that by the mid-eighteenth century, distinct class differences prevailed. Some Carolina planters in the Lower Cape Fear had
amassed large fortunes from exporting naval stores and lumber. Although the households in this region may not have been lavish by the
standards of neighboring colonies, at least half the owners held slaves.
Studies of wealth distribution also show that a small proportion of the
population, both east and west, held a large proportion of the wealth.[5]
Moreover, there is ample evidence to support the contention that North
Carolina's elite, as undeveloped as it may have been, controlled the
public offices of the colony.

The religious profile of the colony made North Carolina decidedly
different from its neighbors. From the very beginning, the proprietors
had encouraged religious freedom, to attract new settlers, and this practice resulted in uncommon diversity. Quakers soon began to move into
the Albemarle region and, by 1700, made up nearly half the population.
In 1701 the Church of England was officially established, but at no time
in the history of the colony was it ever avidly supported. Besides
Quakers and Anglicans, other religious groups in small numbers also
settled in North Carolina. The central area of the colony, occupied by
Germans and Swiss, had Lutheran and Moravian churches. The Scotch-
Irish brought Presbyterianism with them to the west. Small Baptist
organizations were scattered throughout the province. This kind of religious diversity, both cause and effect of what observers called the
people's "indifference" to religion, left the churches with a small role in
colonial affairs.[6]

To some extent, North Carolina's economic circumstances slowed
development. The lack of currency and the lack of skilled labor were
chronic problems. Limited marketable goods hindered overseas trade
while the absence of a valuable resource other than land hampered the
domestic economy. Internal trade was difficult because the few towns
that existed were far apart and because good river transportation was
lacking in the west. North Carolina's economic situation both reflected
and enhanced the colony's regional differences. Albemarle colonists
produced food items and wood products. Their households were typ-

5. Ekirch, *"Poor Carolina,"* 24–29; William Tryon to Earl of Shelburne, March 21,
1768, in *NCSR,* VII, 699; Kay and Cary, "A Demographic Analysis of Colonial North
Carolina," in Crow and Hatley (eds.), *Black Americans,* 111–16.
6. Lefler and Powell, *Colonial North Carolina,* 191–206; Ekirch, *"Poor Carolina,"*
29–30.

ically modest, and they had few slaves. In the Lower Cape Fear region, where, by the 1760s, the majority of the population was black, naval stores, lumber, rice, and indigo formed the economic foundation. Wealth in the colony, though relatively meager, was concentrated here. In the west, where slaveholding was far more unusual, there were many small subsistence farmers.

Political turmoil plagued the Carolina colony nearly from the beginning of settlement. In the early period, Albemarle colonists who had been in the region before the 1660s reacted bitterly to proprietary interference and the influx of new settlers. Slow economic development and extremely ineffective proprietary rule only added to the colony's troubles. Out of such conditions, rebellions are born, and the first came as early as 1677. Sparked by Deputy Governor Thomas Miller's iron hand, Culpeper's Rebellion ended with Miller's removal and his replacement by Seth Sothel, a man whose tenure proved equally destructive. Sothel's harsh rule led to another bitter internal conflict.[7] Finally, in the 1690s, the proprietors imposed some order. They reorganized the colonial government, conferring much greater authority on the assembly. Achieving more independent status, the County of Albemarle came to be known as North Carolina. And the province enjoyed a brief period of harmony and expansion.

But in the early 1700s the Cary Rebellion plunged North Carolina into turmoil once again. Sectional rivalry, factionalism, religious conflict—all were part of this uprising. Trouble began when Governor Thomas Cary sought to undermine the political power of the large Quaker population. When the proprietors tried to replace Cary, he rejected his successor, shifted to the Quaker side, and governed capably for two years. But his rule came to an end when a new governor arrived, and in the unrest that followed, Cary was forcibly sent back to England. The rebellion that bears his name marks a colorful, well-studied episode in Carolina history that is perhaps best explained by undercurrents of sectional conflict. Cary's followers came from newly settled Bath County; their opponents, from Albemarle. Rivals for political power, these two groups clashed in a way that hinted at the kind of regional discord that would be so disruptive. Scarcely had the Cary Rebellion subsided when North Carolinians faced a truly grisly episode. In the

---

7. On Culpeper's Rebellion, see *NCHCR,* II, xxx–lv; on the uprising against Seth Sothel, see *ibid.,* lvii–lix.

space of three days in the fall of 1711, hundreds of Indians from the Tuscarora and allied tribes killed 150 colonists in the newly settled Cape Fear region. The Indians had lashed out brutally, responding to the movement of whites into their lands, particularly the recently established Swiss settlement at New Bern. Lasting four years, the Tuscarora War nearly devastated the colony. During this period the public debt increased, no growth occurred, and thousands died.[8] Yet with all its destructiveness, the war left a colony determined to chart a different course. The bitter factionalism and sectional rivalry of earlier years evaporated for a time as the southern region began to rebuild. Having subdued the Indian population, North Carolina could strengthen and stabilize its affairs. Provincial leaders moved in this direction after the formal separation of North Carolina from the colony to the south in 1712. Three years later the assembly conducted a sweeping review of existing legislation, rejecting some laws, reaffirming others, and passing many new bills that touched on all areas of life.

As North Carolina entered the decade of the 1720s the colony experienced significant growth. This resulted in part from Governor Burrington's opening of the fertile Cape Fear region to development. Burrington may have contributed to the physical expansion of the colony, but he did little to further its tranquillity. His uncontrollable temper and odd behavior helped to renew the factionalism that had been so disruptive in earlier years. His successor, Richard Everard, proved no less contentious.[9] With provincial affairs in complete confusion, and with no prospect of gaining any kind of profit from their venture into colony building, the proprietors finally did what had been expected for a number of years. Seven of them in 1729 sold their shares in the colony to the Crown.

When we look back on the proprietary period, it is not surprising that North Carolina had trouble shedding its frontier beginnings. If not a backward place in 1729, this newly royal colony was still largely rural and had failed to establish the strong leadership and the institutions that would be prerequisites for growth. The proprietors were in large part responsible. They did not create an effective government, work out a

8. On the Cary Rebellion see *NCHCR*, V, xxi–xxii, xxiv–xxv; on the Tuscarora War, see *ibid.*, xxv–xxxii.

9. On Burrington's first administration, see Ekirch, "*Poor Carolina*," 53–57; and *NCHCR*, VI, xxxviii. On Everard, see Ekirch, "*Poor Carolina*," 56–57; and *NCHCR*, VI, xli–xliii.

proper land policy, or appoint able men as leaders. They allowed strong-willed individuals and groups to battle each other for control. These struggles negatively affected North Carolina's governing structure and economic development, and they severely undermined effective law enforcement. In fact, during the Cary Rebellion and the Tuscarora War, government had scarcely functioned at all. Evidence of court activity is scarce. This could be the result of records having been lost, but contemporary comments point to a serious curtailment of legal proceedings. In 1717, for example, a dispute between the governor and the chief justice nearly shut down the colony's highest criminal court for two years.[10] During the 1720s, Governors Burrington and Everard abused their authority by trying to indict their political foes, and North Carolina's transformation to a royal colony only heightened the confusion. While awaiting the arrival of the new royal governor, men in office failed to do their jobs. The official records of the colony are filled with dismaying comments on the political situation. Men spoke of a "suppressed" General Court, of "fallen" precinct courts, and of government that had "sunk so low that neither Peace or Order subsisted." Criminal court activity declined dramatically. Burrington's appointment as the first royal governor did little to stabilize the colony.[11] At a time when "Law & Justice seemed at a stand & but little business done," he was supposed to restore order, to unravel complex land grant problems, and to oversee the collection of quitrents for the Crown.[12] A more capable leader might have succeeded, but Burrington was self-seeking and tactless. His second administration proved to be as stormy as his first. He alienated the assembly, the council, and the chief justice, leading his enemies to carry their attacks to London. In 1733, Gabriel Johnston, a former university professor, replaced him. Johnston immediately set out to rid North Carolina of the factionalism that continued to hinder its progress. Early in his tenure the assembly responded to one of the by-products of rapid population growth in the 1730s—increases in crime and civil litigation—by revamping the colony's legal institutions. But welcome population growth also revived a debate over land policies and, as the governor and the assembly clashed, brought an end to the short-lived political calm. Johnston had stirred up the political waters

10. See *NCHCR*, V, xxxix.
11. Burrington to Duke of Newcastle, July 2, 1731, in *NCSR*, III, 142. On Burrington's second administration, see Ekirch, *"Poor Carolina,"* 54–65.
12. William Little to Burrington, August, 1731, in *NCSR*, III, 200.

by trying to collect quitrents owed to the Crown and by questioning the legality of blank patents involving tens of thousands of acres sold after the proprietors had stopped granting land. Government faltered badly again as the governor and the lower house seemed unable to resolve their differences. Finally, in 1739, they reached a compromise on quitrents and on blank patents, but new issues soon emerged to divide the colony once more.[13]

The main source of discord in the 1740s and 1750s was the rivalry between the older northern counties along Albemarle Sound and the newer southern counties in the Cape Fear region.[14] Inequality in assembly representation, with its origins in the seventeenth century, was one source of conflict. Another was the still undecided location of a permanent seat of government. As both regions vied for a site convenient to them, Johnston inflamed sectional differences by showing favor to the south. He called several assembly meetings there, hoping that the long distance would keep Albemarle delegates away. In fact, they refused to attend the 1746 session in Wilmington, a location favored by the aggressive leaders of the new southern counties. This incomplete assembly passed several bills—to limit representation in the assembly to two delegates from every county, to make New Bern the colonial capital, and to provide new, more central meeting places for the General Court and the circuit courts. Other disputes over paper currency and quitrents added to regional tensions. Trouble brewed especially in the north as delegates continued to boycott the assembly while their constituents refused not only to obey the laws it passed but to pay quitrents and taxes. At times, government in the Albemarle seemed to stop working altogether, creating an atmosphere of "perfect anarchy." "Crimes are of frequent occurrence," noted one uneasy observer there, and "most matters are decided by blows."[15] The colony's highest criminal court, which met in Edenton, practically shut its doors as sheriffs and jurors refused to serve. At the local level, county court proceedings were curtailed drastically. Finally in 1754, the Privy Council moved to unravel North Carolina's tangled affairs by issuing new instructions for the colony.

Since an incomplete assembly had been meeting, all the legislation

13. The best treatment of North Carolina during the royal period is Ekirch, "Poor Carolina." Also see Jack P. Greene, The Quest for Power: The Lower Houses of Assembly in the Southern Royal Colonies, 1689–1776 (Chapel Hill, 1963), 43–45.

14. Greene, The Quest for Power, 337–38.

15. Diary of Bishop Spangenburg, September 12, 1752, in NCSR, IV, 1311–12.

enacted would be repealed. More important, the Privy Council ruled that representation in the assembly should be more equitable and that, for the benefit of the south, the governor should encourage urban growth there. Together with the appointment of Arthur Dobbs as governor following Johnston's death in 1752, these changes were partly responsible for defusing the intense factionalism. Dobbs tried at once to separate himself from his predecessors' divisive policies. He refrained from any particular alliance, thereby earning the praise of the various factions. He also garnered support by trying to lessen the impact of the Crown's renewed interest in colonial affairs. One such effort was his handling of the disallowance of the 1746 court bill.[16] The Crown had rejected the bill in part because an incomplete assembly had passed it. But repeal also reflected a change in British policy. Until 1750, the Privy Council had usually accepted the colonial practice of creating courts by statute. Now the Board of Trade sought to tighten control over the colonies by reminding them that only the governor and the council could establish courts. Dobbs was told "to establish such and so many Courts of Justice as shall appear to be necessary and proper for the better administration of Justice."[17] Not wanting to break with precedent or lose his carefully cultivated support, he allowed the assembly to pass its own court bill to replace the 1746 bill that had been disallowed. At first, the only official response was silence. Then, in 1759, after the supreme courts had been functioning for four years, the Privy Council's painfully slow reaction came. The bill providing for supreme courts was disallowed. This action meant that for nearly a year, until new courts could be established, the colony had no legitimate higher courts. In 1760 the assembly once again passed a higher court measure. But this bill too was disallowed in 1761 because it provided that judges hold office during good behavior rather than during the pleasure of the Crown. The next year the assembly passed a new bill that modified the previous one and left the question of judicial tenure unresolved. Oddly enough, the tenuousness of North Carolina's higher court structure had no perceptible impact on the functioning of the courts. They continued to operate, as usual, while their legitimacy was in question. But the higher court controversy renewed provincial conflict and helped put the governor and the assembly back on a collision course.

16. Greene, *The Quest for Power*, 338–43; Ekirch, *"Poor Carolina*," 125–26.
17. Greene, *The Quest for Power*, 330–32; Board of Trade to Crown, March 14, 1754, in *NCSR*, V, 108; Instructions to Dobbs, March, 1754, in *NCSR*, V, 113.

During the 1760s, the locus of discord shifted from east to west. Attention focused on the Granville District, roughly the northern half of the colony, which was held by Earl Granville as a proprietary.[18] As John Lord Carteret, he alone had retained his proprietor's share of the colony in 1729. Hoping to develop the area, Granville extended unusually generous terms to prospective colonists. He, however, remained in England, leaving the administration of his American estate and the collection of quitrents in the hands of a single, unscrupulous agent, Francis Corbin. Corbin not only encouraged corruption among his land officers, he enraged a large and powerful landowner—Henry McCulloh—by selling property in the Granville District to which McCulloh had legitimate claim. Finally, Corbin charged but never proved that Dobbs was selling property in the Granville District as Crown land. Corbin could not be ignored. He held a seat on the council and was an associate justice. Dobbs removed him from the bench in 1758, and subsequently from the council, but Corbin retained his political influence by appointing assemblymen to lucrative posts as land officers.

Early in 1759, conditions in the Granville District reached a flash point. Angered by the assembly's failure to act against Corbin's corruption, settlers took matters into their own hands. Engaging in what became known as the Enfield Riot, they arrested Corbin and held him for several days. With Corbin's misconduct now exposed, Granville replaced him as land agent in 1759. But Corbin's story was far from ended. He still had powerful friends in the assembly who supported his attempt to prosecute the Enfield rioters. These members of the assembly turned against Dobbs, accusing him of standing silent while the rioters went free. Here at last was an issue that assemblymen could use to send the governor home. They submitted to London fifteen charges against Dobbs, including one that cited his inability to suppress disorder in the Granville District. Dobbs countered by sending his own detailed defense to London. When the Crown upheld his position, his opponents in the assembly backed down. For the next four years, until Dobbs's death in 1765, the governor and the assembly enjoyed a relatively tranquil relationship. His successor, William Tryon, found North Carolina's political leaders united and eager to cultivate his favor. But the corruption and self-interest displayed by the lower house during the Dobbs administration would take its real toll during Tryon's tenure. Although he

18. Ekirch, *"Poor Carolina,"* 133–47.

began his term auspiciously, Tryon was quickly to face a series of disorders capped by the Regulation—the most serious internal strife experienced by the Carolina colony.

Tryon's first major crisis was North Carolina's response to the Stamp Act. Opposition spread throughout the colony, but was sharpest around the Lower Cape Fear region, an important maritime center. Leading citizens there opposed the stamp duties on shipping papers and the requirement that merchant violators of the law be tried by an Admiralty Court in Halifax. Tryon dealt with Stamp Act opponents firmly but cautiously. He first prorogued the assembly for the duration of the crisis, thus effectively removing it as a forum for protest. Early in November, when neither stamps nor stamp master had yet arrived, he suspended all legal and maritime proceedings that required stamped papers. This act shut down the courts, since documents such as writs, judgments, and sentences all required stamps. Virtually no legal or maritime business could be conducted, and when Parliament repealed the law in 1766, not a single stamp had been sold. Ironically, Stamp Act opposition had unified a colony long torn by discord.[19]

Tryon's handling of the crisis earned him praise from colonial leaders who now found little reason to challenge him. But events in the west were about to rock the colony again and in the most threatening way to date. Reacting to the corrupt practices of local officials, Regulators organized themselves in the backcountry counties of Orange, Rowan, and Anson.[20] From 1766 to 1771, hundreds and sometimes thousands of men seeking to "regulate" local government resorted to petitions, tax evasion, disruption of the courts, and violence. Still the topic of debate, the Regulation has been explained as a conflict between east and west,

19. Donna J. Spindel, "Law and Disorder: The North Carolina Stamp Act Crisis," *NCHR*, LVII (1980), 1–16; Tryon to Henry Conway, November 5, December 26, 1765, both in *NCSR*, VII, 122–23, 143–44.

20. As the focus of more scholarly attention than any other episode in North Carolina history, the Regulation has spawned many studies. See, for example, Marvin L. Michael Kay, "The North Carolina Regulation, 1766–1776: A Class Conflict," in Alfred F. Young (ed.), *The American Revolution: Explorations in the History of American Radicalism* (De Kalb, Ill., 1976), 73–123; James P. Whittenburg, "Planters, Merchants, and Lawyers: Social Change and the Origins of the North Carolina Regulation," *William and Mary Quarterly*, 3rd ser., XXXIV (1977), 215–38, journal hereinafter cited as *WMQ*; and Marvin L. Michael Kay and Lorin Lee Cary, "Class, Mobility, and Conflict in North Carolina on the Eve of the Revolution," in Jeffrey J. Crow and Larry E. Tise (eds.), *The Southern Experience in the American Revolution* (Chapel Hill, 1978), 109–51. My interpretation is based on the synthesis in Ekirch, *"Poor Carolina,"* Chap. 6.

between rich and poor, between conservative Whigs and unscrupulous government officials. More recent analyses emphasize the importance of official corruption as a stimulus to Regulator activities. These studies show that many backcountry officials were newcomers to the region and viewed government service as the quickest way to advancement. Ambitious and without scruples, they used their official posts to improve their personal circumstances while they ignored the economic plight of backcountry farmers.

The story of the Regulation has been told many times over. Hermon Husband, a wealthy Orange County settler and assemblyman, led western county settlers in attacks on local corruption and then on the governor and the assembly. Regulators petitioned the government, harassed local officials, and withheld their taxes, all to protest the misuse of public funds. Despite Tryon's firm efforts toward peace, Regulator violence occurred in the backcountry time and again. In 1769, Hillsborough was the site of vicious action. Husband led a large crowd of Regulators to disrupt the Superior Court session, driving judges and lawyers from the courthouse and beating them. Although the governor sympathized with Regulator complaints, he would not allow anarchy to prevail. At his urging, the lower house passed a bill that made it easier to arrest and prosecute rioters. But defiant Regulators continued to disrupt the courts in the western counties and to threaten the lives of court officials. In May, 1771, Tryon answered backcountry protest with force, effectively putting an end to the Regulation. With an army of over a thousand men, he marched toward Hillsborough, where he had called for a special court session to deal with Regulators. Not far from the town, he defeated a larger but poorly equipped force, leaving many casualties on both sides. Tryon's victory at Alamance made him a popular figure in the assembly. Members of the lower house had not been receptive to Regulator charges of corruption among local officials. In addition, those members had themselves become targets of Regulators for their own alleged corruption and abuse of power. While the Regulation began as a crusade to end misconduct among backcountry officials, it eventually spread so wide as to encompass the colonial government itself.

North Carolina leaders publicly praised Tryon for responding firmly to a movement that threatened to undermine entirely the political order. But when he journeyed north in 1771 to become governor of New York, he left behind a long list of Regulator grievances still to be resolved by his successor, Josiah Martin, and the assembly. Martin hoped to enjoy the good will that spilled over from Tryon's administration.[21] But his own study of the cause of Regulator unrest convinced him that there was real substance to their grievances. After personally viewing conditions in the west, he discussed the misuse of power by local officials there. He then proposed to the assembly a judicial reform bill. While scarcely altering the court structure at all, the governor's bill would give him greater control over the selection of justices of the peace and sheriffs. As-semblymen resisted his reform. Taking his criticism of local government as personal attacks on them, they included in their own court bill a measure the governor rejected outright. The assembly had, in fact, sim-ply ignored royal instructions by writing into the bill the power to attach the property of foreigners in debt actions, even if the debtors had never lived in North Carolina.[22] Now with the court bill dead, the entire structure for which it provided broke down. Observers at the time commented on the "curious" and dangerous situation, but the virtual absence of higher court proceedings was brief. To fill the void, Martin created several courts of oyer and terminer without legislative approval. While such courts were not new in the colony, they had been convened in the past by the council, to dispose of a case out of term. With the regular courts now defunct, these special higher courts conducted very little business. They alone prosecuted serious criminal cases until the Revolution.

The much-abbreviated schedule of North Carolina's higher courts was only one of the disruptions during the colony's last years. As much as Tryon had enjoyed the support of provincial leaders, Martin stirred their opposition. His sympathy for the Regulator cause and the debate over judicial reform overlapped areas of conflict between colonial and imperial authority. In previous years, the assembly had formally denied Parliament's right to tax the colonies and had agreed to boycott goods taxed by Parliament.[23] In the summer of 1774, nearly every county sent delegates to a provincial congress meeting in extralegal session, since the governor continued to prorogue the regular assembly. This congress announced its opposition to parliamentary taxation and its determina-tion to suspend trade with Britain. The congress also chose three dele-

21. On Martin's administration, see Ekirch, *"Poor Carolina,"* 203–11.
22. On the higher court controversy of the 1770s, see Greene, *The Quest for Power,* 420–24.
23. On pre-Revolutionary activities, see Lefler and Powell, *Colonial North Carolina,* Chap. 11.

gates to the First Continental Congress in the fall and, most important, created committees of safety throughout the colony to ensure the enforcement of its actions. Governor Martin finally called an assembly into session in April, 1775, hoping to end North Carolina's anti-British actions. Most assembly members then formed an extralegal congress that approved colony-wide protest. Fearing for his safety, Martin fled to a British ship. In his absence, the provincial congress established its own government and prepared for war. Not all North Carolinians resisted British control. Early in 1776 a Loyalist regiment that included a number of former Regulators met Patriot forces at Moore's Creek Bridge. The Loyalist defeat weakened their cause and put off British invasions for several years. Formal independence for North Carolina soon followed. In April, through the Halifax Resolves, the provincial congress supported independence for all colonies. Following approval of the Declaration of Independence, North Carolina set about forming a new government.

North Carolina entered the Revolutionary era in the aftermath of serious internal disorder. Yet provincial strife was nothing new to the colony. And the transition to royal rule proved no remedy for North Carolina's problems. While increased immigration caused expansion south and west, territorial growth and ethnic and religious diversity led to regional conflict and continued political discord. To some extent, the colonial environment allowed factionalism and contention to thrive. Ownership of land was widespread, but the majority of North Carolina's white landowners were relatively poor. Even wealthy colonists lagged behind the richest families of neighboring provinces. With avenues to greater fortunes closed, they advanced themselves through politics. North Carolina's emerging elite ensured their primacy by controlling local government and by holding assembly seats. Official corruption sprang from these conditions and ultimately was most disruptive.

Political unrest, weakened government, official corruption, unfit leaders, slow economic growth, and an expanding slave population, all became the backdrop for the development of North Carolina's law enforcement institutions. Despite the colony's persistent troubles, which by no means made North Carolina unique, two criminal justice systems evolved, built on English and native practices. The Carolina province took from the English system as much as could be reasonably applied in America and built legal institutions for white society that differed in only small ways from those that existed to the north and south. As did other southern colonies, North Carolina created a special court structure to suppress and punish what white society defined as slave crime. The effectiveness of all these institutions depended largely on the particular environment in which they functioned. No colonial law enforcement system faced a greater challenge to its stability and maturation than did North Carolina's. Internal disorders disrupted court activities, suspending criminal court prosecutions for long periods of time. Local resentment and political ambition undermined the reliability of law enforcement personnel. A backwardness in intellectual life and a slow rate of growth until mid-century also affected the enforcement of the criminal law. In addition, North Carolina and the Crown periodically disputed the colony's higher court structure. Furthermore, the population, both black and white, rose rapidly after 1750. All these factors inevitably shaped the contours as well as the control of crime.

II

THE EVOLUTION, PERSONNEL, AND
PRACTICES OF THE COURTS

[T]he Courts so much obstructed
—William Little

The eight original Carolina proprietors laid down their plans for controlling and punishing crime in the proprietary charter, the short-lived Concessions and Agreements, and in the Fundamental Constitutions.[1] These documents reflected the proprietors' desire to create a feudalistic society and, for this reason, were never put entirely into practice. The Fundamental Constitutions provided the framework for the Carolina courts and the foundation for government. Had this Grand Model been followed precisely, law enforcement would have consisted of an elaborate tier of courts and an array of lawmen from stewards to constables. Instead, the criminal courts underwent a number of changes before 1700, each one shaped by the turmoil that so vexed the colony. At the turn of the century, a court system was in place, though nearly forty years later the assembly would make important adjustments in the county courts. Ultimately, North Carolina's courts and law enforcement system reflected proprietary and royal wishes as well as the needs of the colony itself.

From the very beginning of Carolina history, magistrates or summary courts represented the lowest level of criminal jurisdiction. Curiously, they are not mentioned in the official papers of the early colony. In all likelihood, they sat when no higher court was in session.[2] One or two justices of the peace commissioned by the governor convened the court as needed. Since magistrates courts were not courts of record, very little

1. NCHCR, I, 76–89, 107–64.
2. On early magistrates courts, see NCHCR, II, lxix; and Paul M. McCain, *The County Court in North Carolina before 1750* (Durham, 1954).

evidence of their proceedings survives, nor is much known about their authority. Only if a judgment was appealed to the precinct court, a court of record, might the existence of a magistrates court be known. As one of several trial courts in the seventeenth century, precinct courts handled some of the crimes committed in the colony. Every defendant in a precinct court was entitled to "a Jury of his Peers." The Fundamental Constitutions stipulated that the jurisdiction of the precinct courts should extend to the precinct, the colony's smallest administrative unit. On the criminal side, they could "Judge all Criminal causes, except for Treason, Murder, and any other offences punished with death." Composed of five justices commissioned by the governor, each court sat four times a year, usually in private homes. This practice eventually led "to the great Annoyance of the Magistrates and People" and resulted in a 1722 statute that required the construction of a courthouse in each precinct. While precinct courts functioned until 1739, they seldom exercised their authority in criminal matters. Only sixteen criminal prosecutions appear in their records before 1729. Moreover, legislation of 1738, which cites their inability to hear "any Criminal cause or matter whatsoever," certainly suggests that precinct courts rarely tried any criminal cases at all.[3]

For a brief time, from 1683 to 1694, the County Court of Albemarle had the same criminal jurisdiction as was granted the precinct courts. Created by the proprietors in their instructions to the colony, it consisted at various times of the governor, from five to eight justices, and members of the council. Since few records of the County Court survive, it is impossible to know its exact role in early law enforcement.[4]

In 1691, as part of the reorganization of the colonial government, the proprietors replaced the Fundamental Constitutions and called for a modification of the existing court structure. The General Court, which had functioned since the 1670s in various forms, remained the highest court in the colony. Although not mentioned specifically in the Constitutions or in the governors' instructions, this court was made up of the governor and the council. Meeting three times a year in Edenton, the General Court had original and appellate jurisdiction over all criminal matters. Beginning in 1698, the governor and the council no longer

3. *NCHCR*, I, 183, 144–45; act of 1722, *NCSR*, XXIII, 100–102; act of 1738, Colonial Office, Ser. 5, Vol. 333, typewritten transcript in North Carolina State Department of Archives and History, Raleigh, repository hereinafter cited as NCA.
4. *NCHCR*, II, lxiii–lxiv.

served automatically on its bench. Instead, six or seven justices were commissioned by the governor and the council. Two were usually councillors, and these men were always among the three judges in quorum. In this way, North Carolina departed from a practice that Virginia followed throughout the colonial period—creating the highest court from the governor and the council. Perhaps the proprietors sought to free council members for the business of governing. Virginia councillors, to be sure, were too busy in later years to hold the circuit courts that became the linchpin of the Carolina system. North Carolina's highest court also differed from those in northern colonies. In Rhode Island and Connecticut, for example, the assemblies filled all judicial posts.[5]

In 1715 the assembly recognized the presence of perhaps one thousand slaves in the colony by establishing courts to try slaves accused of crimes. Much like slave courts in the British West Indies and in other southern colonies, these courts consisted of "any three Justices of the Precinct Court where such Offence or Crime shall be Committed & three Freeholders such as have Slaves in that Precinct." There was no grand jury or trial jury. The bench was to "have full power & authority" to hear and determine "& to pass Judgment for life or Member." Herein legislators created a legal means of depriving blacks of rights traditionally extended to all English men and women accused of crimes. The objective was simple—to keep the slave population, small though it was, under absolute control. Punishment was to be swift and public. Unruly slaves would learn by example to obey. Nor did the assembly lose sight of the fact that slaves who committed crimes were also property. Masters would be compensated through "a Pole-Tax on all Slaves" for those executed or "killed in Apprehending."[6]

When North Carolina became a royal colony in 1729, the immediate effect on the criminal courts was negligible. Magistrates courts continued to have the same authority in criminal matters they had had in previous years while the precinct courts and the General Court remained the same. In 1730, however, the Crown instructed Burrington, the first royal governor, to appoint two courts of oyer and terminer "for

    5. NCSR, I, 373–80; Scott, Criminal Law in Colonial Virginia, 47–48. See Edward M. Cook, Jr., The Fathers of the Towns: Leadership and Community Structure in Eighteenth-Century New England (Baltimore, 1976), 154; and Joseph H. Smith (ed.), Colonial Justice in Western Massachusetts, (1639–1702): The Pynchon Court Record (Cambridge, Mass., 1961), 82–88.
    6. Kay and Cary, "A Demographic Analysis of Colonial North Carolina," in Crow and Hatley (eds.), Black Americans, 72; act of 1715, NCSR, XXIII, 62–66.

the better prevention of long imprisonment." The next year he commissioned the chief justice, council members, and assistant justices of the General Court to hold this special court. North Carolina governors continued to issue these commissions irregularly throughout the colonial period, but not always to clear the jails. There were special courts in the 1760s to try Regulators and again in the 1770s to replace the higher courts that the Crown had disallowed.[7]

North Carolina's new royal status initiated a period of expansion that by the end of the 1730s was straining its law enforcement institutions. As population grew in the northeastern precincts a single provost marshal (or chief law enforcement officer for the colony) could not do his job effectively.[8] To remedy "the great delay of Justice" and to ensure that justice was "more effectually administered," the assembly in 1738 replaced the provost marshal and his deputies with a sheriff in each county and changed the name of precinct courts to county courts. Since the precinct courts' limited jurisdiction had resulted in "divers petit Larcenies and other misdemeanours [being] Pass'd over with Impunity," the assembly augmented the county courts. Beginning in 1739, justices of the peace exercised the same authority as did the "Justices of the Quarter Sessions" in England. Meeting four times a year, they could "hear and Determine all Petit Larcenys, Assaults, Battery, Breaches of the Peace and Behaviour, and all Misdemeanors and Crimes of an Inferiour Nature" by information, grand jury indictment, or presentment. Following the English practice, defendants in the county courts had "the right to bring a Certiorari or other Process to remove the Proceedings" to the General Court in Edenton. Every county court had a deputy prosecutor appointed by the attorney general of the colony. Grand and petit juries, made up of male freeholders, would be summoned by the sheriff of each county to serve in the county court. Although the Fundamental Constitutions set the freehold requirement at fifty acres, the legislation does not specify the size of the freehold that qualified a man for jury service.[9]

Seventy years after the founding of the colony, lower courts were finally granted clear and definite jurisdiction over lesser crimes. Begin-

7. Instructions to Burrington, December 14, 1730, *NCSR*, III, 105; council meeting, November 23, 1731, *ibid.*, 256.

8. See David L. Corbitt, *The Formation of the North Carolina Counties, 1663–1943* (Raleigh, 1950), xvii–xviii.

9. *NCSR*, XXIII, 122; act of 1738, CO 5/333; freehold requirements, in *NCHCR*, I, 145.

ning in 1739, county courts became important social and legal institutions, handling not just people's everyday civil affairs but their misbehavior as well. The criminal authority of the county courts never changed, even when, in the years to come, the higher courts were shaken by political strife. Nor did the makeup of the judges' bench alter over time. And for as long as these courts existed, a criminal suspect entering this bedrock of local law enforcement could seek a jury trial.

The court bill of 1738 also made changes in the higher court structure. By then, it was apparent that the three meetings per year of the General Court in Edenton, which alone had jurisdiction over serious crimes, were no longer adequate for a colony spreading south and west. The "great Distance of the several Counties" from the court's meeting place created "Difficulty and expence of Travelling thither . . . and of Bringing and Proving Witnesses." When these circumstances led to "many great and enormous crimes . . . committed with Impunity," the assembly established three circuit courts "of Assize oyer and Terminer and General Gaol Delivery" to hear causes that arose in the counties named for each circuit. The chief justice of the Edenton General Court rode the circuit, appearing twice a year in Bath, New Bern, and Newton (later Wilmington), where he acted "according . . . to the method us'd and Practised by the Judges of Assize in England." The General Court continued to meet in Edenton to try criminal actions that arose in the Edenton district. As was true in England, where assize justices actually received three commissions, the chief justice could hear and determine "all Treasons Murders Burglarys Felonys Trespasses" and "try all Persons against whom any Indictments shall be found or Presentment made or Information exhibited."[10] Notably missing from the 1738 statute was a provision for the English practice of issuing a commission of oyer and terminer to justices of the peace along with assize judges. This omission no doubt reflected a desire to keep local justices, whose criminal case experience was minimal, from hearing felonies.

The new circuit courts had grand and petit juries of freeholders from any or all of the counties in each district. According to legislation that had been in effect since 1723 and that was partially based on a provision in the Fundamental Constitutions, a special procedure was followed in choosing jurors. At the end of each court session, a child not older than ten pulled from a box "the Names of twenty four persons" who ap-

10. See J. H. Baker, "Criminal Courts and Procedure at Common Law 1550–1800," in Cockburn (ed.), *Crime in England,* 27.

peared on a list of eligible jurors included in the legislation. The sheriff summoned these men to appear at the next meeting of the court. If more than twelve came, a child selected the jury by drawing from a box that contained the names of those present. If fewer than twelve came, the sheriff could choose jurors from among the eligible freeholders who happened to be there.[11]

North Carolina's circuit court plan differed from those in other southern colonies. Virginia had previously created similar courts, but they existed only briefly. All the reasons that apparently discouraged such courts in Virginia—long distances to travel, lack of professional judges, a small number of felony cases—applied to North Carolina as well. Nor did the centralized South Carolina criminal courts offer a model for the North Carolina assizes. New York circuit courts were somewhat similar, though its Supreme Court had a permanent location and the justices held yearly circuit courts.[12] Yet circuit courts in early North Carolina served a twofold purpose. The three new circuits helped develop the communities in which they met. This was true especially for the recently settled southern town of Newton. More important, the Carolina assizes strengthened law enforcement that the colony's size and the dispersal of the population had weakened.

In 1741, Carolina legislators took great pains to adjust to two recent developments—the frightening Stono Rebellion, and the burgeoning slave population in their own colony. While the previous legislation on freeholders courts (1715) had said virtually nothing about procedure, now the law was quite clear. Borrowing again from the laws of neighboring colonies, the assembly empowered a justice of the peace to commit a slave offender to the jail in the county where the crime occurred. The sheriff would then "Certify the same to any Justice" in the county. This justice would bring the court together—at least three judges and four freeholders who owned slaves. Once again, no jury sat in a freeholders court. Admissible evidence included "the Oath of one or more credible Witnesses, or such Testimony of Negroes, Mulattoes or Indians, bond or free." Owners could come to court to defend their accused slave. If a slave was executed, the assembly provided compensation. Legislators

11. *NCSR*, XXV, 184–90.
12. See Scott, *Criminal Law in Colonial Virginia*, 47–48; M. Eugene Sirmans, *Colonial South Carolina: A Political History, 1663–1763* (Chapel Hill, 1966), 251; and Julius Goebel, Jr., and Thomas R. Naughton, *Law Enforcement in Colonial New York: A Study in Criminal Procedure, 1664–1776* (1944; rpr. Montclair, N.J., 1970), 26–30.

altered the statute on slave courts three more times, but the court's makeup and procedures remained the same.[13] Slaves accused of crimes would have none of the safeguards afforded their white counterparts. Justice would be quick and brutal. The criminal courts would be one more tool of repression in a slave society.

Until 1746, trials for whites charged with serious crimes were held at the General Court in Edenton or at one of the circuit courts. But continued growth and new political troubles led to changes in the circuit. Responding in part to the increasing influence of colonists from the southern counties, the assembly transferred the General Court from Edenton in the north to the more centrally located New Bern. The assize or district courts would meet in Edenton, Wilmington (formerly Newton), and the Edgecombe courthouse. These courts did not function for long—the bill providing for them was disallowed in 1754.[14]

In 1748 the assembly tried to remedy the serious problem of finding enough jurors for the district courts. From this time on, defendants faced juries chosen not by sheriffs or by chance, but by justices of the peace and grand juries. When this new method of securing jurors proved no more effective than the old had been, the assembly directed justices of the peace in each county to elect by majority vote half the jurors and the grand jury to choose the other half. In 1760, legislators tried one last time to deal with absent jurors by instructing justices of the peace alone to name jurors. Certainly no more galling problem presented itself to the Carolina courts than that of insufficient juries. No matter how much the General Assembly tinkered with juror selection and penalties for absenteeism, incomplete juries continued to challenge effective law enforcement.[15]

Assembly action in 1754 altered the framework of the higher court system but made no substantive changes. The statute eliminated the General Court and assize courts, divided the colony into five judicial districts, and created five supreme courts equal in authority with jurisdiction over the counties in their respective districts. The supreme courts, which had the same criminal authority as did the supreme court or the General Court they replaced, were convened twice a year by the

13. Act of 1741, *NCSR*, XXIII, 191–204. See acts of 1753, 1758, 1764, *ibid.*, 388–90, 488–89, 656.

14. *NCSR*, XXIII, 252–67. See David L. Corbitt, "Judicial Districts of North Carolina, 1746–1934," *NCHR*, XII (1935), 45–61. On the political motives for the court transfer, see Ekirch, "*Poor Carolina*," 91–94.

15. Act of 1748, *NCSR*, XXIII, 289–91; act of 1749, *ibid.*, 330; act of 1760, *NCSR*, XXV, 422–24.

chief justice and three associates at their seats in Edenton, Enfield (moved to Halifax in 1758), New Bern, Salisbury, and Wilmington. The purpose of the change was to lessen the distance officers, jurors, and "suitors" of the higher courts had to travel to attend. Soon after these supreme courts had begun to operate, the law providing for them, which included a controversial measure on the appointment and qualification of judges, was disallowed by the Crown. In 1760, one year after the disallowance, the assembly created a superior court system basically identical to the supreme courts. But this act was disallowed in December, 1761, because it stipulated contrary to the wishes of the Crown, that judges hold office during good behavior. Anxious now to create some form of higher courts, the assembly in 1762 passed a superior court bill that said nothing about judges' tenure and that reduced the number of associate justices in each district from three to one. Until 1773, the higher court laws remained in effect briefly and were then renewed with minor changes.[16] Governor Martin did not renew the court bill in 1773 because the assembly included a measure he opposed. Martin then commissioned several courts of oyer and terminer, exercising his right to do so without legislative approval. One such court had been held in May, 1771, to try Regulators, and these special bodies, which met irregularly from 1773 to 1777, represented the last of the higher criminal courts to operate in colonial North Carolina.[17]

It may be that no other colony experienced the repeated changes in the court system that plagued North Carolina after mid-century. Too much should not be made of this, however, because the changes were, on the whole, ones of form rather than function. With its origins in the seventeenth century, the General Court provided an institutional foundation on which the later higher courts could be built. Despite frequent efforts to establish acceptable and permanent higher courts, the General Assembly still managed to preserve the crucial element of continuity.

The justice of the peace was a key figure in the control of crime in the colony. Within his county, he symbolized the law enforcement system.

16. Act of 1754, *NCSR*, XXV, 274–87; act of 1760, *ibid.*, 433–39; act of 1762, *NCSR*, XXIII, 550–63. On the tenure of judges, see Greene, *The Quest for Power*, 341–42.

17. Josiah Martin to Earl of Dartmouth, April 6, 1773, in *NCSR*, IX, 626–32. On the attachment bill controversy, which led to the failure of the court bill, see Don Higginbotham (ed.), *The Papers of James Iredell* (Raleigh, 1976), I, lix–lx; and *NCSR*, IX, xxiii–xxiv. On special courts, see Address of Governor Martin, December 4, 1773, *NCSR*, IX, 708.

In North Carolina his authority derived from a commission of the peace, issued by the governor and the council, and from statutes. The justices of the peace provided for in the Fundamental Constitutions were substantial landowners, holding three hundred acres. Dating from 1679, the earliest surviving commission authorized justices of the peace to preserve the peace in their jurisdictions according to the laws of the colony or, in the absence of such laws, the laws of England. The Carolina justice was to be a man "of Substance and Ability of Body and Estate; of the best Reputation, good Governance, and Courage for the Truth." He was a magistrate, an examining officer, a judge of the county court, and the chief police officer of his county.[18] Early on, a justice of the peace acting alone exercised limited authority in criminal matters. He responded to complaints by ordering suspects to be brought before him for a hearing, by binding them over to the next session of the court with jurisdiction, or by settling the case himself. In 1715 the assembly augmented and clarified his duties. In a sweeping revision of the colony's legal system, the Carolina justice was made more like his English counterpart. He now protected moral standards by uncovering and punishing immoral behavior. He fined drunks, swearers, and those he observed misbehaving on Sunday. Two justices together could examine and fine unmarried, pregnant women, bind over the fathers to the precinct courts, and compel suspected unmarried couples to produce a marriage certificate. Acting in court, at least three justices of the peace could try petit larcenies, assaults, trespasses, breaches of the peace, and misdemeanors. And together with freeholders they could conduct a summary court to try slaves suspected of crimes.[19]

A number of historians give low marks to justices of the peace, particularly those in the Carolina backcountry. This assessment is certainly not contradicted by the few surviving commentaries of the period.[20] In 1709, missionary William Gordon caustically remarked that "the people indeed are ignorant, there being few that can read, and

18. Fundamental Constitutions, NCHCR, I, 144; NCHCR, II, lxvii–lxviii; James Davis, The Office and Authority of a Justice of Peace (Newbern, 1774), 226.

19. NCSR, XXIII, 3–6; Davis, Justice of Peace, 229; act of 1715, NCSR, XXIII, 62–66.

20. For negative comments on colonial justices, see Clement Eaton, "A Mirror of the Southern Colonial Lawyer," WMQ, 3rd ser., VIII (1951), 524; A. G. Roeber, Faithful Magistrates and Republican Lawyers: Creators of Virginia Legal Culture, 1680–1810 (Chapel Hill, 1981), 58, 119; Greenberg, Crime and Law Enforcement in New York, 175; and Ekirch, "Poor Carolina," 171.

fewer write, even of their justices of peace." The assembly expressed
dismay in 1733 about the need "to prevent so many Evil Magistrates
from being appointed as We find there hath been these few past years."
Indeed, a number of eighteenth-century justices of the peace appeared in
criminal courts before the bar rather than behind it. Consider the case of
William Gray, a Bertie County justice charged with assault, or of
William Yancy, a justice from Tryon County, convicted of petit larceny.[21] How exceptional were these cases? A list of 1,272 local judges,
gathered from many different sources, contains the names of 122 justices accused of misbehavior either before, during, or after their tenure
on the bench.[22] Surely a certain amount of judicial misbehavior would
be expected in a colony still in the early stages of its development. What
is puzzling is that official misconduct was not a common charge against
accused judges. Extortion appears only five times. Blatant misbehavior,
generated by alcohol, perhaps, or plain incompetence, was rare. The
actions of Peter West, prosecuted for giving "an oath to several persons
in very obscene terms," or Robert Read, "for losing the Crown Docket,"
or James Washington, for "abusing the position," were not the norm.[23]
A typical charge against a local judge might be assault, trespass, or
ordinary swearing. Murder charges accounted for only three; serious
assaults, sixteen; and serious thefts, five. Nor do the records indicate
that a handful of evil justices committed all the crimes. Nearly all justices were criminal suspects only once. In short, there is no evidence to
suggest that the number of criminal suspects among North Carolina
justices was so large as to undermine their overall effectiveness.

21. William Gordon to Secretary of State, May 13, 1709, in *NCSR,* I, 712; General
Assembly message to Upper House, July 14, 1733, *NCSR,* III, 595; *Crown* v. *Gray,*
November, 1763, Edenton District Court Records, 1763–64, *Crown* v. *Yancy,* October,
1771, Tryon County Court Minutes, 1769–74, both in NCA.
22. The list of justices of the peace was compiled from original documents and the
published records of the colony. Criminal suspects among them were identified by comparing names on that list to names on a list of all criminal suspects; by comparing the county
served with the county in which the alleged offense occurred; and by comparing the years
served on the bench with the year in which the prosecution took place. The total figure—
1,272 individual justices and 122 criminal suspects among them—is, at best, conservative. Names that could not be verified through those comparisons were discarded.
Identical names were counted as a single person unless separate identities could be
established.
23. For Peter West, see Council Journals, March 16, 1743, *NCSR,* IV, 626; *Crown* v.
Read, March, 1776, Carteret County Court Miscellaneous Court Dockets, 1775–1843,
NCA; *Crown* v. *Washington,* July, 1746, General Court Criminal Papers—General and
Assize Courts, 1745–49, and General Court Dockets, 1746–47, NCA.

Criminal court data also bring into sharper focus the misdeeds of backcountry justices, a topic of real interest in studies on the origins of the Regulation. With the exception of some of the more notorious lawmen such as Edmund Fanning, backcountry officials seem to have evaded prosecution for their misdeeds. This fact alone underscores the depth of their control of the courts. Patterns of prosecution against justices of the peace, which are regionally correlated, reveal that backcountry justices were no more inclined to be criminally charged than were justices in other counties. Between the 1750s and the 1770s, nine justices from Rowan County and nine from Granville County allegedly committed crimes; so did nine from Craven County, eight from Tyrrell, and seven from Hyde during the same period. Moreover, backcountry judges generated the same mix of criminal charges as did those serving in eastern counties.

Measuring the overall ability of justices of the peace is a task fraught with complications, not the least of which is the lack of reliable documentation. At the very least, it makes sense to delve into the extent of their legal knowledge. Given the slow pace of development in North Carolina, in both economic and intellectual life, it is hardly surprising that few local judges were formally trained in the law.[24] Although some acted as counselors for criminal defendants, it is impossible to say how much legal understanding they brought to the courtroom.[25] Yet the lack of a formal legal education by no means made them an "ignorant lot." Carolina judges showed the same "industry" and "zeal" that New York justices of the peace were known for. And, like their Virginia counterparts, they must have absorbed some legal knowledge from the world in which they lived and worked.[26] In 1715 the General Assembly required that a "book of Laws . . . shall be constantly laid open upon the Court table during the sitting of the Court." Some justices owned the same abridgments of English statute and case law found in the libraries of

24. Two North Carolina justices before 1776 had studied at the Inns of Court—Thomas McGuire and Gabriel Cathcart. See E. Alfred Jones, *American Members of the Inns of Court* (London, 1924).

25. For example, Thomas Barker, Bertie County justice of the peace, often acted as a counselor in criminal trials during the 1730s. John Hodgson, a Chowan County justice, acted as defense counselor in the General Court.

26. See Goebel and Naughton, *Law Enforcement in Colonial New York*, 137; and Warren M. Billings, "English Legal Literature as a Source of Law and Legal Practice for Seventeenth-Century Virginia," *Virginia Magazine of History and Biography*, LXXXVII (1979), 406–407.

seventeenth-century Virginians. Included among the more than five hundred volumes in Samuel Johnston's library were thirty-four "books devoted to the theory and practice of law . . . and various collections of colonial laws." Among these were works by Coke and Blackstone. The bookplates show that many of these books had been owned by other justices of the peace. North Carolina justice Robert Turner listed "law books" in his will, as did Edward Salter, Jr., and Edward Moseley. Other judges had copies of such standard works as "an Institution of the Laws of England," *Laws of Virginia,* the writings of Coke, Hawkins, and Wood, the *Attorneys Pocket Book,* and Webb's *Justice of the Peace.* In 1749 the assembly elaborated on earlier legislation by instructing justices to buy "the latest Editions of the Law Books following, to wit: Nelson's Justice, Cary's Abridgement of the Statutes; Swinburn of Wills, or Godolphin's Orphan's Legacy, and Jacob's Law Dictionary, or Wood's Institutes."[27]

Laymen's legal manuals, popular in other colonies, no doubt taught Carolina lawmen the fundamental rules of the job. Michael Dalton's *The Countrey Justice* and Swinburne's *Brief Treatise of Testaments,* both widely used in Virginia, probably circulated to the south. Justice John Eustace had a copy of Nelson's *Justice* in his library; and William Whitehead, a copy of Webb's *Justice of the Peace.* These manuals describe in alphabetical order the duties of local lawmen, give instructions for prosecuting crimes, and contain copies of required legal forms. They are also filled with references to English and colonial statutes, as well as terse quotations from previously published works. A Virginia manual, published by George Webb in 1736, became the model for North Carolina's own guide, written and printed by James Davis in 1774.[28] Davis' background, in and of itself, shows that at least some of North Carolina's justices had a long, intimate acquaintance with the law. He served as a justice of the peace in Craven County for twenty years and a member of the assembly for five.

North Carolina justices had many opportunities to acquire legal

27. Act of 1715, NCSR, XXIII, 95; Billings, "English Legal Literature," 403–16; Stephen B. Weeks, "Libraries and Literature in North Carolina in the Eighteenth Century," American Historical Association, *Annual Report for the Year 1895* (Washington, D.C., 1896), 203; J. Bryan Grimes, *Abstract of North Carolina Wills* (Raleigh, 1910); Grimes, *North Carolina Wills and Inventories* (Raleigh, 1912); Helen R. Watson, "The Books They Left: Some 'Liberies' in Edgecombe County, 1733–1783," *NCHR,* XLVIII (1971), 245–57; act of 1749, NCSR, XXIII, 346.
28. Billings, "English Legal Literature," 414; Roeber, *Faithful Magistrates,* 118–19.

knowledge through experience. Data gleaned from the court records, the published records of the colony, and manuscript sources show that 1,266 justices of the peace intermittently served twenty-nine counties between 1720 and 1776. Nearly half (626) served one or two years; 943 (74.5 percent) served five years or less. While their tenure does not seem to parallel that of Virginia justices, long terms were not unusual.[29] Two hundred twenty-four (17.7 percent) served six to ten years; 68 (5.4 percent) were justices of the peace for eleven to fifteen years. Many justices moved in and out of office, interspersing their service with terms in the assembly, and sometimes even serving in both posts concurrently. While 811 (64.1 percent) were never assembly members, 351 (27.7 percent) served in the assembly for one to five years, and 189 (14.9 percent) acted simultaneously as justices and assembly delegates for the same period of time. In fact, in each of the thirty assembly sessions, from 1722 through 1776, more than half of the delegates had been or would become justices of the peace.[30] Besides occupying the bench of the county courts and holding seats in the assembly, 49 also saw service as associate justices of the higher courts.

The extensive government service of North Carolina justices of the peace confirms a conclusion reached by other studies—that judicial positions were tied to plural office-holding, and that this phenomenon enabled local judges to exercise and solidify their power.[31] Not only did they move in and out of official positions, but some families regarded these offices as a vested right. A list of all known Carolina judges, in the period from 1720 through 1776, contains 754 different surnames. Of the 215 names that appear more than once, 85 percent occur fewer than five times. Although the judicial ranks were never as inbred as Virginia's, 32 surnames appear at least five times or more.[32]

Drawn as sharply as it can be, the picture of the judicial system at the

29. On office holding by Virginia justices, see Hoffer and Scott (eds.), *Criminal Proceedings in Colonial Virginia,* xviii–xix; and Charles S. Sydnor, *American Revolutionaries in the Making* (1952; rpr. New York, 1965), 76.

30. This figure was determined by cross-referencing a list of justices of the peace culled from the court records with listings of assembly members in John Cheney, Jr. (ed.), *North Carolina Government 1585–1974* (Raleigh, 1975), 33–57.

31. See William S. Price, Jr., "'Men of Good Estates': Wealth Among North Carolina's Royal Councillors," *NCHR,* XLIX (1972), 75; Lefler and Powell, *Colonial North Carolina,* 219; and Kay and Cary, "Class, Mobility, and Conflict," in Crow and Tise (eds.), *The Southern Experience in the American Revolution,* 137.

32. Examples of surnames that occur five times or more are Alston, Bryan, Harvey, Lane, Moore, Sumner, and Ward.

county level shows a relatively small and powerful group of men, some of whom shared government positions and some of whom were members of the same families. From all indications, these men represented North Carolina's political elite. They were not legal scholars, but they could acquire knowledge of the law through their culture, available printed works, and experience. Within their counties, these men could be powerful indeed. Outside the courtroom, they collected evidence, heard testimony, and generally kept the peace. Inside the courtroom, they wielded considerable authority in such areas as procedure, sentencing, fining, and settling bonds for good behavior. Ultimately, the respect that their authority brought them helped make the system work.

Men and women accused of serious crime faced not the familiar bench of the local courts but the chief justice of the colony and his associates. The proprietors created the office of chief justice in 1712, and the chief justice was commissioned by them. Between 1720 and 1776, there were fourteen men who occupied this position, some of them serving at one time or another as attorney general, justice of the peace, and member of the assembly. They were, for the most part, men prominent in the colony who had years of experience in government. In 1767, Governor Tryon described the chief justice as "an officer of dignity, trust and importance . . . there is lodged in him all the powers and authorities vested in . . . the courts of Kings Bench . . . in England."[33] Associate justices were appointed by the governor and the council. The seventy-eight men who served, between 1720 and 1776, were to be "of good life and . . . of good estates and abilities and not necessitous persons," though they were not, as were their English counterparts, meant to be a professional judiciary.[34] Of good estates they were—such prominent families as Allen, Blount, Campbell, Gale, Harvey, Moore, and Pollock were well represented on the bench of the higher courts. Some associate justices—Thomas McGuire, James Murray, and Robert Palmer, for example—were also men of substantial wealth.[35]

Like their counterparts in the lower courts, associate justices probably had little formal legal training. Unlike the relatively well trained judges in other colonies, only two Carolina men studied at the Inns of

33. *NCHCR,* V, xxxviii; Cheney (ed.), *North Carolina Government,* 58; Tryon to Earl of Shelburne, June 29, 1767, in *NCSR,* VII, 477.

34. Instructions to Burrington, December 14, 1730, in *NCSR,* III, 92. A list of associate justices was compiled from references in *NCSR* and the court records.

35. Price, "'Men of Good Estates,'" 79.

Court. Some associate justices were lawyers, meaning that the governor had licensed them to practice. But only the one who presided at the Salisbury District Superior Court needed a license. Because the place was remote, he typically held court without the chief justice and could exercise all his powers. The government did not require formal training for other associates, since "their offices are purely honorary attended with no profit worth mentioning."[36] Their jurisdiction was limited to their district, and in the absence of the chief justice, their power was restricted. This explains, in part, their brief terms of office—81 percent served only one to three years. Yet as a group, these men still represented years of varied public service. They supplemented their judicial posts with terms as justices of the peace and as assembly members and councillors.[37] Nearly 63 percent had been or would become justices of the peace, 40 percent served in the assembly before or after their judicial term, and 44 percent had been or could expect to become councillors. Roughly one-quarter were associate justices and justices of the peace the same year, and 26 percent held simultaneous positions as associate justices and assembly members. This kind of multiple office-holding, so typical at the time, not only filled their pockets but also gave them at least a rudimentary education for the job. By mid-century, though, associate justices were not men on the make, but men who were already there. Their place on the bench attested to their prominence and signaled, at least in part, the entrenchment of a governing elite.[38]

Attorneys represent a group whose role in law enforcement is difficult to gauge. Derisive contemporary comments certainly call their effectiveness into question. In 1732, for example, Governor Burrington complained about "Several ill Disposed persons under pretense of being attorneys without being duly Qualified." This remark is understandable, since lawyers were among Burrington's most bitter political foes.

36. Cook, *The Fathers of the Towns,* 155; Paul M. Hamlin and Charles E. Baker (eds.), *Supreme Court of Judicature of the Province of New York* (New York, 1959); Tryon to Earl of Shelburne, June 29, 1767, in *NCSR,* VII, 477. Eight of the lawyers listed in Ernest H. Alderman, "The North Carolina Bar," in *James Sprunt Historical Publications,* edited by J. G. de Roulhac Hamilton and Henry M. Wagstaff (Durham, 1913), XIII, 7, served as associate justices.

37. A list of seventy-eight associate justices was cross-referenced with a justice of the peace file and a list of assembly members and councillors in Cheney (ed.), *North Carolina Government,* 10–23, 33–57.

38. See Ekirch, *"Poor Carolina,"* 82–83; and Kay and Cary, "Class, Mobility, and Conflict," in Crow and Tise (eds.), *The Southern Experience in the American Revolution,* 137–38.

The governor's own attorney, David Osheal, allegedly "abused and libelled" a jury in 1732 when it reached an unfavorable verdict. Nor did the reputation of lawyers appear to improve with the passage of time. In 1760 the assembly expressed dismay at the granting of "Licences to Persons to Practice the Law who are Ignorant even of the Rudiments of that Science." Indeed, the route to obtaining a law license was not, by modern standards, a particularly hard one. Any man could practice if he had "taken the degree of Outer Barrister in some of the inns of court," or if upon "a perfunctory examination" and recommendation by the chief justice, the governor granted him a license. In 1767, Governor Tryon noted that most North Carolina attorneys who practiced law had licenses. Presumably, they had passed a review of their legal knowledge and integrity.[39]

Even if some attorneys were ignorant of the law, they could, like justices of the peace, learn through experience, or apprenticeship, or from books. Some received a more formal education. John Burgwin studied at Oxford and Cambridge, Marmaduke Jones somewhere in England, and John Dunn at Oxford. Samuel Ashe and Eleazer Allen attended Harvard, Thomas Barker acquired legal training in Rhode Island, Alfred Moore studied in Boston, and William Hooper was at Harvard.[40] Apprenticeship was a more likely route. When Samuel Johnston asked Thomas Barker to take his son as an apprentice, Barker replied that the boy was "welcome to the use of my books and to my advice in reading them." William Hooper studied under James Otis, Samuel Ashe with his uncle Samuel Swann, Alfred Moore with his father, and James Iredell with Samuel Johnston.[41]

A number of attorneys, such as Samuel Johnston, John Hodgson, and

39. Ekirch, "Poor Carolina," 25; Directive of Governor Burrington, April 3, 1732, General Court Minutes, 1732, NCA; Crown v. Osheal, October, 1732, General Court Criminal Papers, 1730–34, NCA; House Resolutions, May 23, 1760, NCSR, VI, 411; Alderman, The North Carolina Colonial Bar, 6; Tryon to Earl of Shelburne, June 29, 1767, in NCSR, VII, 485.

40. Burgwin and Jones: Crocket W. Hewlett, Attorneys of New Hanover County (New Hanover, 1976); Dunn: Rev. Jethro Rumple, A History of Rowan County, North Carolina (Salisbury, 1881), 69; Ashe: John Wheeler, Reminiscences and Memoirs of North Carolina (Columbus, Ohio, 1884), 301; Allen: Hewlett, Attorneys of New Hanover County; Barker: William S. Powell (ed.), Dictionary of North Carolina Biography (Chapel Hill, 1979–), I, 96; Moore and Hooper: Hewlett, Attorneys of New Hanover County.

41. Thomas Barker to Samuel Johnston, May 26, 1753, in Hayes Collection, Southern Historical Collection, University of North Carolina Library, Chapel Hill; Hewlett, Attorneys of New Hanover County; Wheeler, Reminiscences, 301.

William Hooper, had substantial law libraries. James Milner left in his will at least one hundred law books, including Webb's *Virginia Justice,* the *Attorney's Pocket Companion,* and the works of Coke, Hawkins, Hale, and Blackstone. If the self-education of James Iredell is any indication, licensed attorneys were reading Bacon's *New Abridgement of the Law,* the first part of Coke's *Institutes,* and Blackstone's *Commentaries.* Attorney Waightstill Avery studied history as well as Goldbolt's *Reports—Statutes at Large* and Fitzherbert's *Natura Brevium.* And while riding the circuit in 1769, Avery dined with lawyers, drank with them, traveled with them, and argued with them over points of law. In 1767, North Carolina boasted forty-five licensed attorneys. As Avery did, these men rode the circuit, in effect selling their skills like wares. They seemed to form a coterie of "professionals" whose legal education was no better or worse than that of practitioners elsewhere. Virginia lawyers, for example, were examined by barristers of the General Court and by attorneys selected by the governor and the council. In New York, regulations were more stringent. By 1767, the Supreme Court there would only recommend attorneys who had served as clerks for five years or for three years if they had a college degree. In contrast, the Massachusetts requirements for the practice of law were largely informal until the 1760s. Much of the later regulation, which came from the colony's own bar associations, was similar to that of other colonies.[42]

The routine and the sometimes dangerous tasks of law enforcement, such as apprehending and arresting suspects, fell largely to the sheriffs and constables. Until 1739, the most important lawman in the colony was a provost marshal, appointed by the governor and assisted by a deputy in each precinct. When poor performance "occasioned great Murmurs and Discontents among the Inhabitants," the assembly abolished the office of provost marshal and placed a sheriff in each county. Every two years thereafter, county courts gave the governor a list of three justices of the peace. The governor selected one man from the list to serve a two-year term as sheriff. The new appointee, who could not succeed

42. Weeks, "Libraries and Literature of North Carolina," 206–207; Grimes, *North Carolina Wills,* 516; Higginbotham (ed.), *The Papers of James Iredell,* I, 56; "Journal of Waightstill Avery," *North Carolina University Magazine,* IV (1885), 253–55; Tryon to Earl of Shelburne, June 29, 1767, in NCSR, VII, 486; Roeber, *Faithful Magistrates,* 121; Paul M. Hamlin, *Legal Education in Colonial New York* (1939; rpr. New York, 1970), 39–40; Gerard W. Gawalt, *The Promise of Power: The Legal Profession in Massachusetts, 1760–1840* (Westport, Conn., 1979), 12.

himself, gave up his place on the bench. A sheriff was not meant to be an ordinary citizen. Indeed, he had to be a man of some means, since the law required him to post a bond of at least £500. In theory, he also had to be a man of some energy. Sheriffs had innumerable responsibilities, for which they received a fee set by law. They executed writs, maintained the public accounts, arrested suspects, subpoenaed witnesses, kept prisoners, carried out sentences, periodically attended the General Court and "constantly" attended the county court, and summoned juries and filled them out, if necessary, with bystanders. In his demanding capacity as "principal Conservator of the Peace within his County," the sheriff also broke up fights and helped suppress riots. If offenders resisted or tried to flee, he could kill them.[43]

Sheriffs were liable for their negligence. Between 1737 and 1747, charges of extortion were made against five sheriffs, though none was convicted.[44] Studies of later years, buttressed by critical contemporary remarks, suggest that sheriffs, particularly in the western counties, were a bad lot who freely embezzled funds. This negative view of Carolina sheriffs sounds a familiar chord in the colony's history, though recent research points to the need for some revision. From an eighteenth-century perspective, this job was not in high demand. Why give up a prominent place on the bench for the time-consuming and probably thankless job of sheriff? Many men paid a fine rather than serve. By 1745, sheriffs were in such short supply that the assembly accepted any "well qualified" person for consideration. With earlier restrictions removed, unscrupulous men may then have sought the post.[45]

The most routine and ordinary tasks of law enforcement fell to the constable, a citizen policeman who, by design, had much the same background and community status as did the people he served. Appointed by the county court, he put up no bond, but needed only to be "discreet." More prominent members of the community—justices of the peace, clergymen, lawyers, and physicians—were purposely ineligi-

43. Act of 1738, NCSR, XXIII, 122; Davis, Justice of Peace, 331.
44. Crown v. Bell, February, 1737, General Court Criminal Papers, 1735–37, and General Court Docquet, July-October, 1739; Crown v. Phelps and Crown v. Cheney, March, 1745, General Court Criminal Papers—General and Assize Courts, 1745–49, and General Court Dockets, 1745–46; Crown v. McDowell, March, 1745, Crown v. Person, July, 1747, General Court Criminal Papers—General and Assize Courts, 1745–49.
45. Ekirch, "Poor Carolina," 157; Alan D. Watson, "Sheriffs in Colonial North Carolina," NCHR, LIII (1976), 385–98; act of 1745, NCSR, XXIII, 218.

ble.[46] The constabulary drew the humbler elements of a community into the peace-keeping system. During their one-year term, constables performed an array of tasks that would stagger the imagination of the modern-day policeman on the beat. Constables executed warrants and took suspects into custody, keeping them in their own home if necessary. They attended the county court to assist with the grand and petit juries. As "Conservator of the Peace," a constable broke up fights and quarrels, disarmed anyone carrying a weapon "in Terror of the People," suppressed riots, and apprehended "Rogues, Vagabonds and idle Persons." How well these civilian law enforcers performed their tasks is difficult to say. Some paid fines for failing to appear in court. A few were charged with negligence.[47] But the tens upon hundreds of returned writs in the records of the county courts tell a story of rather remarkable diligence. Consider the experience of William Turner in his pursuit of a suspected thief in 1727. Turner submitted a bill to the county court for his expenses incurred in "6 days in apprehending, waiting, Guarding & bringing him [the suspect] to Prison, having 2 men & myself constantly waiting upon him. . . . 1 day coming & 1 Day going from Court. . . . 5 days attendance as Evidence." This suspect apparently did not challenge his arrest, but others did. Constables routinely faced strong resistance from suspects, some of whom had higher community standing than did the lawmen. Their travails are among the most colorful and dismaying stories the court records have to tell. For example, Constable John Simpson in 1723 tried to arrest a planter named Robert Atkins. The suspect shouted at him to "kiss his own Arse" and drove him off with "Servants & doggs . . . sticks staves & weapons."[48]

In view of the demanding and thankless aspects of their job, it is perhaps to be expected that few constables extended their one-year term. In a sample of 227 appointees taken from the court records for the 1663-to-1740 period, 90 percent served for one year, and the remaining 10 percent for two. Many of them doubtless found the job a real burden,

46. Act of 1715, *NCSR,* XXIII, 15–16; Davis, *Justice of Peace,* 116.
47. Duties of constables: Davis, *Justice of Peace,* 118–23. Constable fines: March, 1740, Craven County Court Minutes, 1730–46; and December, 1774, and June, 1775, Rowan County Court Records in Salisbury District Court Trial and Minute Docket, 1761–90, NCA. Constable negligence: *Crown* v. *Daniel,* October, 1743, General Court Criminal Papers, 1740–44; *Crown* v. *Morgan,* October, 1757, General Court Criminal Papers—General, Assize, and Supreme Courts, 1750–59.
48. Account of William Turner in General Court Criminal Papers, 1720–29; *Crown* v. *Atkins,* March, 1724, *NCSR,* II, 544–45.

one that interrupted their lives for a year and also compelled them to discipline friends and neighbors. But if they lacked motivation or skill, constables may still have been aided by their familiarity with the people and communities they served.

When a crime occurred, if it was swearing, drunkenness, or bastardy, justices of the peace could handle it out of sessions. For more serious offenses, they issued arrest warrants based on their own knowledge of a crime or on information someone gave to them. These warrants were executed by a sheriff or a constable who held the suspect for a hearing before a local judge. At this hearing, the judge examined the suspect and took depositions from witnesses and victims. If he found sufficient evidence, he bound over witnesses and prosecutors to the next meeting of the court that had jurisdiction. Suspects could be admitted to bail, following the practice outlined in the English statutes, but those who were not bailable stayed in jail, at least in theory, until the court met.[49]

On the opening day of court, the grand jury convened, witnesses arrived, and a constable was assigned to attend the private grand jury deliberations. Grand jurors could consider indictments based on an earlier examination before a justice of the peace. They could also present suspects who had not appeared before an examining court but who they believed had committed a crime. If at least twelve grand jurors found the evidence convincing, the clerk wrote *Billa vera* (true bill) on the indictment. If they found the evidence defective, he wrote *Ignoramus* (we ignore the bill) and the suspect was discharged. When the grand jury indicted suspects, the clerk issued a *Capias* against them. This document instructed the sheriff to bring them before a local judge who would bind them by recognizance to appear at the next session of the court with jurisdiction.

A true bill did not always signify a trial. Defendants could, of course, plead guilty, though they did not commonly do so in the Carolina courts. Occasionally, the accused "Submitted himself to the mercy of the Court," apparently a confession and a plea for leniency. Sometimes prosecutors entered a *nolle prosequi,* discontinuing the indictment. This could happen for many different reasons, though the records rarely tell us what they are. One unusual but predictable example comes from the General Court of 1728, which entered nine different charges *nolle pros-*

49. Acts of 1715 and 1741, *NCSR*, XXIII, 3–6, 173–75; Davis, *Justice of Peace,* 39–49.

equi because they "had laine before the General Court for a Considerable time." One of the defendants was George Burrington, a man always
at the center of political strife in the 1720s. If a *nolle prosequi* did not
end an indictment, a motion to quash could. Again, court clerks usually
recorded the motion without any explanation for who initiated it or
why. A defendant's influence, a technical error in the proceedings, insufficient evidence, or new information in the case—any or all of these
could explain the motion. Consider the experience of George Allen, a
frequent defendant in the General Court during the 1720s. His two
attorneys persuaded the court to quash a presentment against him by
pointing out errors in the indictment.[50]

A criminal defendant could have his day in court only after the court
finished its civil business. Procedure then required arraignment and trial
first for men and women accused of lesser crimes who had asked to be
judged by God and country at the previous session of the court. Most
defendants entered the courtroom without counsel at their side. In fact,
English law permitted counsel only in less serious cases, "unless some
doubtful Point of Law arise." In theory, the judge protected the defendant's rights and made sure he received a fair trial. In practice, North
Carolina courts duplicated what had been accepted in Virginia since
1734, and allowed accused felons to have counsel. According to James
Davis in his 1774 manual for justices of the peace, "Prisoners may have
Council" when being tried for capital crimes.[51] In practice, few criminal
defendants had counsel, even in felony cases. And among those who
did, there seems little correlation with status. Attorney Thomas Barker,
for example, counseled Nicholas Tart and Thomas McKeel, planters, in
their General Court trial for theft in 1736. John Hodgson, a familiar
counselor in the General Court, defended Daniel Hamner, gentleman,
against a libel charge the following year. At the same time, men of lesser
means also had legal help. Thomas Jones aided William Roads, a la-

50. *Crown v. Martin* and *Crown v. Ross,* July, 1727, NCHCR, VI, 421; Goebel and
Naughton, *Law Enforcement in Colonial New York,* 591–97; *Crown v. Burrington et al.,*
November, 1728, in *NCSR,* II, 817; appearance of George Allen, July, 1726, NCHCR, VI,
278. Also see *Crown v. Williams,* March, 1741, General Court Docket, March-July-
October, 1741; *Crown v. Worthington,* June, 1755, Hyde County Court Appearance,
Crown, Reference, and Prosecution Dockets, 1744–61; *Crown v. Allen,* August, 1764,
Carteret County Court Dockets, 1764–75.

51. J. S. Cockburn, *A History of English Assizes, 1558–1714* (Cambridge, England,
1972), 121; Giles Jacob, *Law Dictionary* (London, 1750); Scott, *Criminal Law in Colonial Virginia,* 79; Hugh F. Rankin, *Criminal Trial Proceedings in the General Court of
Colonial Virginia* (Charlottesville, 1965), 89; Davis, *Justice of Peace,* 136.

borer, in a 1735 murder trial. Nicholas Fox counseled George Nixon and Thomas Nixon, laborers, when they pleaded innocent in 1738 to stealing and killing a steer.[52]

Unfortunately, even when it is apparent that counselors are present at trials, virtually nothing is said about what they actually do. Insights into actual courtroom proceedings are rare. One unusual example is the case of Christian Newton, a single woman, who pleaded guilty to larceny. Newton begged the court for mercy, citing her youth, and her "Council" argued that her crime was the result "of her youthfull folly." The fascinating diary of lawyer Waightstill Avery opens a window briefly on a 1769 criminal trial at the Rowan County courthouse. In his defense of Paul Crosby, indicted for petit larceny, Avery "Was opposed by all the Atty's at the Bar." Attorney Samuel Spencer "spoke an Hour and 11 minutes. Then I answered him, & spoke to all the Law & Evidence, that any way affected the Cause at Bar, in an Hour & 5 minutes.—Major Dunn closed with a plea or rather loose Declamation, 3 Hours & 17 minutes. When the Jury went out and soon returned their verdict, not guilty. And immediately I was surrounded with a flood of Clients and employed this term in no less than 30 actions." This passage is remarkable for what it says about courtroom procedure and about jury deliberations. In a single day, attorneys' arguments absorbed more than five hours of Crosby's trial, after which the jury retreated only briefly to its chambers. In this case, Avery made a difference. Perhaps that is why he discussed the case, with obvious pride, in some detail. His success certainly brought him many more clients—whether the charges were criminal or civil we do not know. Suggestive as Avery's account is of the decisive role an attorney could play, the evidence, or lack of it, is on the side of a minor role. Defendants usually looked to the bench for "Counsel; and the behaviour of the prisoner in his own Defence, is one Means of discovering the Truth."[53]

When a felony defendant approached the bar, he heard his indictment for the first time and was asked to make a plea. If he confessed, the clerk recorded his words "and no more done till Judgment." Sometimes

52. *Crown* v. *Tart* and *Crown* v. *McKeel*, March, 1736, General Court Criminal Papers, 1735–37; *Crown* v. *Hamner*, March, 1737, General Court Criminal Papers, 1735–37, and General Court Docquet, July-October, 1739; *Crown* v. *Roads*, October, 1735, General Court Criminal Papers, 1735–37; *Crown* v. *George Nixon and Thomas Nixon*, January, 1738, General Court Criminal Papers, 1738–39.

53. *Crown* v. *Newton*, July, 1728, NCHCR, VI, 506; "Journal of Waightstill Avery," 254; Jacob, *Law Dictionary*.

a defendant and the accuser reached an agreement before pleading, which allowed the defendant to plead guilty and pay "a small Fine." Unfortunately, guilty pleas are rarely accompanied by an explanation. Laborer William Hughes, for example, in 1727 stood accused of three different offenses. The record of his case tells us that he pleaded not guilty to the first two charges, "but being called to the Barr a Second time in Order for his Tryall he pray'd leave to withdraw his plea aforesayd which being granted he then pleaded Guilty and humbly moves the Court for mercy."[54] Although we do not want to infer too much from this scant bit of information, it may be that Hughes plea-bargained for a lighter sentence. The Carolina records give every indication that men and women claiming innocence did not seek bench trials, as was the practice in Virginia, but put themselves upon "God and Country."[55] At this time, the clerk called witnesses and the jury was impaneled. A defendant could challenge as many as thirty-five jurors. It was fairly common in the county court for justices of the peace to serve on the jury—a practice known in England. Nor was it unusual for the same jurors to sit in several or all criminal trials during a single court session.[56]

The court heard evidence for the prosecution first, after which the defendant might question witnesses and call his own as well. "When the Prisoner hath done . . . the Evidence is summed up by the Court to the Jury."[57] The jury then retreated to "Some convenient Place" to de-

54. Davis, *Justice of Peace*, 325, 323; *Crown v. Hughes*, October, 1727, NCHCR, VI, 456–57.

55. Hoffer says that in Virginia many defendants chose to put themselves "upon the court," thereby allowing the justices to determine guilt or innocence. There may have been bench trials in North Carolina, but the records do not leave that impression. Colonists who avoided trial did so by pleading guilty. The waiving of a jury trial apparently occurred in some colonies, but not in others. See Hoffer and Scott (eds.), *Criminal Proceedings in Colonial Virginia*, xxii, xxx. Also see Susan C. Towne, "The Historical Origins of Bench Trial for Serious Crime," *AJLH*, XXVI (1982), 123–59; and John M. Murrin, "Magistrates, Sinners, and a Precarious Liberty: Trial by Jury in Seventeenth-Century New England," in David D. Hall, John M. Murrin, and Thad W. Tate (eds.), *Saints and Revolutionaries: Essays on Early American History* (New York, 1984), 156. Langbein suggests that it was not common practice in England to waive a jury trial, since by confessing or seeking a bench trial, the accused lost the chance to enable a jury to downgrade his offense. See John H. Langbein, "Shaping the Eighteenth-Century Criminal Trial: A View from the Ryder Sources," *University of Chicago Law Review*, L (1983), 121.

56. William Hawkins, *A Treatise of the Pleas of the Crown* (1724–26; rpr. New York, 1972), II, 414; Cockburn, *A History of English Assizes*, 112, 251–52; NCSR, II, 463–67; November, 1757, Salisbury District Court Minutes, Superior Court, 1756–70, NCA.

57. Davis, *Justice of Peace*, 327.

liberate without food or drink. When the jurors returned and announced their verdict, a convicted defendant came before the bar for
sentencing. A number of options were then available to him. In the
county courts, a convicted offender could appeal to the higher court,
though there is little evidence that this occurred often.[58] He could also
claim benefit of clergy, a special form of pardon. Serious offenders such
as counterfeiters were denied this privilege. Once granted benefit of
clergy, the prisoner would "be burnt on the . . . left Thumb with the
Letter T. as a Mark to prevent his being allowed Clergy a second Time."
The surviving court records show that the Carolina courts granted
clergy only twenty-nine times to individuals convicted of either theft or
murder.[59]

Convicted defendants could also avoid a sentence by a pardon, arrest
of judgment, or acquittal from the verdict. Granted by the governor,
these actions were allowable in all cases but "Treason & Wilful
Murder." For these two crimes, the governor could grant a reprieve
while awaiting the will of the Crown. But governors seldom interfered
with local justice because they seldom granted pardons.[60] Nor were the
courts necessarily merciful when they did. Often a defect in the process
separated a prisoner from his sentence. A "wicked and malicious" prosecution led to a reprieve for murderer James Powell in 1736.[61] Yet, all in
all, Powell was one of the fortunate few. Most prisoners, once a sentence
was pronounced, could expect to suffer it. Without counsel, their own
limited knowledge of the law offered them the narrowest of options.
Alone at the bar with the bench as their guide, they could count on only
the most flagrant errors in the process to help them avoid their fate.

By modern standards, a colonial criminal trial began and ended in
the blink of an eye. It was, in fact, the norm for several trials to take place
on the same day and for a single jury to hear every one. At its January

58. On appeals, see Davis, *Justice of Peace,* 12; *NCSR,* III, 107; and act of 1746,
NCSR, XXIII, 265. For examples of cases appealed to higher courts, see *Crown* v. *Baker,*
October, 1725, *NCSR,* II, 602; *Crown* v. *Gint,* November, 1769, Salisbury District Court
Trial and Minute Docket, 1761–90; and *Crown* v. *Munroe,* May, 1774, Rowan County
Court Minutes, 1773–86.
59. Davis, *Justice of Peace,* 105. For examples of prisoners granted clergy, see *Crown* v.
Atkins, March, 1740, General Court Papers, 1740; *Crown* v. *Bently,* June, 1768,
Wilmington District Court Minutes, Superior Court, 1760–83, NCA.
60. Instructions to Governor Burrington, January 15, 1730, *NCSR,* III, 70; Instructions to Governor Dobbs, February, 1761, *NCSR,* VI, 528. For examples of pardons, see
Crown v. *Purcel, Keel, and Luard,* December, 1738, *NCSR,* IV, 337.
61. *Crown* v. *Powell,* October, 1736, *NCSR,* IV, 223.

session in 1754, an Onslow County court busily heard and disposed of at least five cases. In 1757 the Salisbury District Court session handled seven separate criminal trials, three of which were settled in a single day.[62] James Cumberland, for example, heard his indictment for felony on Tuesday, was tried and convicted on the same day, and then was sentenced to hang on Thursday.[63] Trials such as this proceeded quickly, once witnesses and defendants appeared, because there was little to delay them. Records of court cases that contain the names of witnesses show that few came to testify. The absence of a defense attorney no doubt hastened a trial, as did the defendant's prospect of paying court costs. And finally, since the courts did not sit continuously, judges pressed forward to clear their dockets.

In theory, the Carolina courts were to act justly, without malice or bias. Every justice of the peace pledged to "do equal Right and Justice to the Poor and to the Rich."[64] In practice, the structure of the system and the kind of men who ran it worked against fairness, at least by modern standards. But criminal law does not function in a vacuum. As the law reflects the society that creates it, the law establishes a code of conduct that judicial personnel must enforce. In this way, criminal behavior was not only defined by the privileged but punished by them as well. At the local level, prominent justices of the peace tried to preserve the social order as they perceived it in their own communities by carrying out their roles as police and judges. In the district courts, judges could more easily distance themselves from the defendants who came before them and could react to crime as it affected not localities, but rather the colony as a whole. Ironic as it may seem, colonial judges carried a heavy burden of responsibility. Often they were the best line of defense against an unfair trial. And they need not have been ignorant men. They could and did in fact learn what they had to from books, conversation, and experience. They did not need sophisticated knowledge of the law to handle the routine misbehavior that occurred.

In assessing the justness and the competence of early Carolina law enforcement, we must resist making twentieth-century comparisons. Could defendants be judged by a jury of their peers when major seg-

62. Onslow County Court Crown Docket, 1753–55; May, 1757, Salisbury District Court Minutes, Superior Court, 1756–70.

63. *Crown* v. *Cumberland,* June, 1756, Salisbury District Court Minutes, Superior Court, 1756–70.

64. Davis, *Justice of Peace,* 228.

ments of the population were excluded from jury service? Could a suspect put his trust in a jury that heard other cases besides his own and that heard all the evidence and reached a verdict in a single day? Or could men ably conserve the peace when witnesses and suspects ignored subpoenas and when bystanders in the courtroom substituted for absent jurors? These were routine practices in the Carolina courts. And these practices, seen through the lens of history, created a distinct form of criminal justice. The terms *fairness* and *justness* can apply to a particular context. Indeed, when applied to the operation of the freeholders courts, they take on a new meaning altogether. These courts were established without any point of reference in the English tradition. They were created to perpetuate oppression, not to sustain the English definition of order and stability in a white world. There could be little that was subtle in the "justice" these courts meted out. Nuances of class, status, and perhaps even gender did not exist. Yet these courts show that racial slavery was ever present in the Carolina world. How the freeholders courts and the regular courts evolved and worked reveals much about the culture that produced them.

III

CRIME IN THE CAROLINA COLONY

[N]ot having the fear of God before her Eyes
—Crown v. Branch (1721)

At the General Court in Edenton, in October, 1727, a laborer named William Hughes confessed that he had stolen "two Handkercheifs One Old Ozenbriggs Shirt One Old Hatt One payr of Silver shirt Buttons one payr of Gaitres One Ivory handle Knife and fork two Small bunches of white tape a Bottle with Some Rum and one Knitt Capp." Just two years later the same court convicted Solomon Smith, also a laborer, of stabbing a man to death with "One mortall wound in and upon his left breast . . . about One inch and half long and about five inches in depth." An ordinary theft and a violent killing—these extremes of criminal activity appear in the court records time and again. In and of themselves, they reflect the underside of colonial life and identify for us today precisely those behaviors that put the stability of the eighteenth-century world in jeopardy. Unfortunately, the colonists were not given to expressing their private thoughts on crime. Only occasionally do the records contain references to "rogues" and "thieves" or comments on the increase in certain crimes, especially when political strife disrupted the courts. Lacking helpful native observations, we should look to English legal scholars, whose works the colonists knew, for contemporary perceptions of crime. Blackstone defined crimes as actions that not only harmed individuals but also "strike at the very being of society." If such actions went unpunished, society could not survive. To prevent the shattering of social bonds, to maintain the "tranquility of the whole," governments created laws and ensured their enforcement by punishing men and women who defied them. In the strictest sense, not every violation of the law was a crime. Only misbehaviors "of a deeper and more atrocious dye" were actually called crimes. All the rest, all "the smaller faults and omissions of less consequence," were misdemeanors. More than any other factor, the degree of intent distinguished a "crime" from a "lesser act."[1] Since men and women were essentially corrupt, crime occurred when they failed to restrain their baser tendencies. Some failed more miserably than others did. For the sake of convenience, no distinction will be made here, except as noted, between crimes and lesser acts. The word *crime* is loosely used to encompass the array of misdeeds that filled the records of the Carolina courts.[2]

Legal definitions of crime in North Carolina varied little from those in England. Lawmakers applied the mother country's statute and common law to their own situation as much as possible. Now and then the assembly enacted its own criminal statutes to deal with slave and servant crime, moral misbehavior, or criminal acts that were on the rise. During the whole span of the colonial period, North Carolinians recognized at least forty-five different kinds of misbehavior. These actions are divided here into felonies and misdemeanors, terms borrowed from Wood's *Institute*, a required text in the Carolina courts. Felonies were serious crimes "for which a capital punishment . . . was liable to be inflicted" or lands or goods forfeited.[3] By the mid-eighteenth century, less serious offenses came to be called "misdemeanors." These were infractions the penalties for which were by fine, corporal punishment, or forfeiture of goods.[4]

Theft was the most commonly prosecuted felony (Table 1). The seriousness of the theft depended on the value of the stolen goods and how they were taken. If the court assigned a value greater than twelve pence, and the items were not taken directly from a person or a house, the crime was simple grand larceny, a felony tried by the higher courts. If the value of the goods was less than twelve pence, and the theft occurred in the

1. *Crown* v. *Hughes*, October, 1727, *Crown* v. *Smith*, March, 1729, NCHCR, VI, 456, 569; Sir William Blackstone, *Commentaries on the Laws of England* (1765–69; rpr. New York, 1979), IV, 5–7; Herrup, "Law and Morality," 110.

2. Throughout this study, in order to "cast the widest net," I included in measurements of criminal prosecutions all bills brought before the grand jury—no bills as well as true bills. See Michael S. Hindus and Douglas Lamar Jones, "Quantitative Methods or *Quantum Meruit*? Tactics for Early American Legal History," *Historical Methods*, XIII (1980), 68.

3. Thomas Wood, *An Institute of the Laws of England* (London, 1724), IV, 340; Blackstone, *Commentaries*, IV, 94.

4. Wood, *An Institute*, IV, 396–97.

TABLE 1

CRIMINAL ACTIONS, BY COURT, 1670–1776

				Percentage Prosecuted		
Crime	Number	1670–1754 General Court	1679–1776 County Court	1755–1759 Supreme Court	1760–1772 Superior Court	1773–1775 Oyer and Terminer
Assault	1,299	18.32%	51.04%	6.31%	23.02%	1.31%
Theft	522	36.02	29.50	6.51	25.29	2.49
Crimes against morality	340	24.41	67.05	0.29	7.35	0.58
Trespass	246	12.20	52.03	6.50	25.61	3.66
Animal stealing	217	27.19	25.35	2.76	41.04	3.69
Contempt	145	54.48	22.06	4.14	19.31	—
Crimes against public order	130	20.76	13.07	6.92	56.15	2.30
Homicide	111	54.95	—	9.91	31.53	3.60
Other[1]	1,098	22.58	48.08	2.64	23.67	2.73
Total	4,108					

NOTE: The actions include presentments and indictments.

[1]Includes 29 different offenses (472 total charges) plus an additional 626 charges that are not identifiable in the records.

same way, the crime was simple petit larceny, a less serious felony tried by the county courts. If a thief violently stole from a person or a house, the crime was robbery, a capital offense. Stealing from a house by breaking into it at night was burglary, also a capital crime.[5]

Since the higher courts prosecuted the majority of thefts (70 percent), most such crimes were of the more serious sort. Yet the court records describe stolen goods that, by modern standards, seem paltry. A stolen hat and knife brought John Lewis into court in 1695. Three years later a jury convicted Anthony Dawson of breaking into a deserted ship and stealing "two Firkins of Butter two cheeses two Casks of vinager to the value of forty shillings." In 1725 the General Court accused James Pottar of stealing a drinking glass, six sheets of writing paper, and one basin from George Burrington. A laborer named Robert Spring allegedly carried off a featherbed (an item indicative of wealth in England), and William Ward was charged with stealing thirty yards of cloth.[6] In general, the items that appear time and again on felony indictments include barrels of corn or pork, shoes, linen, plates, currency, and bills of credit. These goods were valuable or scarce, were needed by the poor, or could be hidden or traded for cash. Their very meagerness shows starkly that in a developing colony of vast land area and a small but growing population, there was not that much worth stealing.

Animal stealing was a particular form of felonious theft that was common and that occupied a separate category in the records. It should come as no surprise that colonists lost cattle, pigs, and horses to thieves, since raising livestock was an important part of the economy.[7] Few material goods of value and the difficulty of protecting livestock made farm animals a tempting target.

Colorful and distressing are the accounts of those crimes that involved colonists showing contempt for authority. This typically felonious act included speech disrespectful to government, resisting arrest, and abusing a magistrate. The case of Julius C. Parke, who challenged an arrest by William Arkill, deputy sheriff for Chowan County, shows how defiant North Carolinians could be. When Arkill tried to take him into custody, Parke "being mounted on his Horse and

5. Ibid.; Blackstone, Commentaries, IV, 223–47.

6. Crown v. Lewis, November, 1695, NCHCR, II, 210; Crown v. Dawson et al., March, 1698, NCHCR, III, 197; Crown v. Pottar, 1725, General Court Criminal Papers, 1720–29; Crown v. Spring, August, 1739, General Court Criminal Papers, 1738–39; Crown v. Ward, July, 1743, General Court Criminal Papers, 1740–44.

7. Merrens, Colonial North Carolina in the Eighteenth Century, 134.

Armed with Sword and pistolls did rid violently towards him and said Damn his blood he would not go before the said Chief Justice and used divers threatening Speeches against the said Chief Justice." Laborer Michael Wattson challenged a lawman in 1746 when he picked up "a Large Stake & Swore the Killing any one Should Come to him." John Brooks allegedly showed contempt by stealing official papers. Solomon King, perhaps in a fit of rage or inebriation, pulled down a courthouse door.[8] Other men and women, acting much as colonists did elsewhere in America, resisted tax collectors and overseers of roads, abused constables, and assaulted sheriffs and justices of the peace.

No one committed a more despicable act than felonious homicide, not only violating "the laws of nature" but also endangering "all civil society." Grand juries charged some with murder, always punishable by death, and trial juries convicted them of manslaughter, an offense "within the benefit of clergy," or chance medley, a killing in self-defense. In 1743 a grand jury indicted Charles Dent, charging that Elinor Dent, infant, "by the Barbarous Cruel and ill treatment of Charles Dent her father . . . Languished" for several days and died. Deciding that he had not willfully killed her, the trial jury found him guilty of manslaughter, for which he was burned on the hand. Quarrels between husbands and wives sometimes had lethal consequences. John Powell was convicted of poisoning his wife. Richard Miller told several justices that "he knockt [his wife] on the head and Killed her with a paddle by giveing of her Two Blows on the head" after an argument. Other murder charges highlight a cruel double standard of justice in a slave society. In 1743, Matthew Hardy attacked his slave Lucy "with stocks and staves," then tied her to a "Ladder extended and with straw and other combustible matter set in fire roasted and burned [her]." According to the records of the case, Hardy was discharged. Only in 1774 in North Carolina did a white person's killing a slave become murder.[9]

8. Complaint of William Arkill, January 19, 1740, General Court Criminal Papers, 1740–44; *Crown v. Wattson*, July, 1746, General Court Criminal Papers—General and Assize Courts, 1745–49; *Crown v. Brooks*, November, 1738, General Court Criminal Papers, 1738–39; *Crown v. King*, March, 1742, General Court Criminal Papers, 1740–44.

9. Blackstone, *Commentaries*, IV, 176–77; *Crown v. Dent*, July, 1743, General Court Criminal Papers, 1740–44; *Crown v. Powell*, July, 1736, General Court Criminal Papers, 1735–37; Examination of Richard Miller, April 16, 1700, *NCHCR*, III, 388; *Crown v. Hardy*, October, 1743, General Court Criminal Papers, 1740–44. See Don Higginbotham and William S. Price, Jr., "Was It Murder for a White Man to Kill a Slave? Chief Justice Martin Howard Condemns the Peculiar Institution in North Carolina," *WMQ*, 3rd ser., XXXVI (1979), 596–97.

Infanticide was another form of homicide so especially painful to discover in the records, but one that in fact rarely resulted in prosecution. In 1735 the General Court, sensitive to a mother's grief and despair, acquitted Ann Morris of killing her five-day-old son by stuffing his mouth to quiet him. A single woman, Morris possibly killed her child as she tried to hide him. In 1744 a grand jury failed to indict Ann Sumner, also single, on the charge that she "did make an assault and the said Bastard Child being alive with her hand round the neck of the said Living child feloniously . . . then and there strangled; of which the aforesaid female Bastard Child instantly dyed." One notorious case involved Mary Gorman, a twenty-year-old woman who apparently disguised herself as a servant, Tom Savage, during her pregnancy and secretly delivered her child on board a ship where she worked. According to the ship captain, John West, Gorman told him, "I am a Woman kind & went to the End of the House and Opened her Jackett and shewed me one of her Breasts." On the night the child was born, West had noticed Gorman's bloody sheets. When the body of an infant was found washed ashore, he made the connection.[10]

A long list of misdemeanors fills the records of the Carolina courts, but assault was the most common. This particular offense, which conjures up an image of a bloody and brawling colonial world, was by definition "an Attempt to Do a Hurt to One's Person tho' no Hurt Actually Done."[11] If a person made an assault "in a forcible Manner, with Intent to commit Roberry," it then became a felony and would be tried by a higher court. Unfortunately, the records have little to say about why people did battle with each other. Many of these episodes no doubt arose from quarrels within families or among friends, from drunkenness, or from arguments over money. Consider a 1743 session of the General Court, busy with assault prosecutions. The grand jury presented Margaret Arkill, a planter's wife, and Nicholas Cullinton, a tailor, for assaulting each other on the same day. These charges never went to trial, but Arkill also assaulted Elizabeth Cullinton, perhaps the wife or daughter of Nicholas, for which she was fined one shilling. An argument over delivery of goods or payment of a bill may have driven

10. *Crown* v. *Morris*, October, 1735, General Court Criminal Papers, 1735–37; *Crown* v. *Sumner*, March, 1745, General Court Criminal Papers—General and Assize Courts, 1745–49; Examination of John West, August, 1726, General Court Criminal Papers, 1720–29.

11. Wood, *An Institute*, IV, 423. Assault was also the most commonly prosecuted misdemeanor in Virginia. See Hoffer and Scott (eds.), *Criminal Proceedings in Colonial Virginia*, liv.

Mary Osbrough and Agnes Osbrough to accuse William Williams, hatter, of assault in 1762. Time and again the records give the impression that personal arguments erupted into violence. In 1745, Media White attacked Thomas Rogers, who was himself accused of attacking Media White three months later. In 1762, Anthony Hutchins and George Downs accused each other of assault, as did James Nicholas and David Henricks in 1764. Some people may have been naturally contentious, the target of malicious neighbors, or caught up in the swirl of political strife. George Allen faced assault charges five times in two years. A few prosecutions for fighting are revealing for what they hint at. The indictments against bricklayer Peter Young for assaulting Sarah Arnold, against John Sanders for attacking Martha Sumner, and against Stevens Lee for abusing Lidia Bay suggest the cruelty of master to servant or man to woman.[12]

As much as North Carolinians seemingly resolved their differences in a physical way, they also engaged in behavior that violated the moral prescriptions of their world. At a time when the laws of God served as a basis for the laws of men, sinful acts were crimes. Responsibility for protecting the people's moral welfare rested squarely upon the government. In England, church courts had jurisdiction over moral offenses so long as they were not cognizable at common law. In America, the assemblies enacted statutes to establish moral standards, and the quarter sessions largely enforced them. One of the many bills passed by the North Carolina assembly after the division of the colony in 1712 identified a number of sinful acts and their penalties. Noting that "Impiety is likely to grow to a very great height, if not timely prevented," the assembly prohibited "Prophane Swearing & Cursing," the "loathsome Sin of Drunkenness," fornication, adultery, and bastardy. Breaking the Sabbath was also an offense, as was operating a tavern without a license or

12. Jacob, *Law Dictionary*; *Crown v. Arkill* and *Crown v. Cullinton*, October, 1743, General Court Criminal Papers, 1740–44, and General Court Docket, March-July-October, 1743; *Crown v. Arkill*, July, 1743, General Court Criminal Papers, 1740–44, and General Court Docket, March-July, 1744; *Crown v. Williams*, September, 1762, Salisbury District Court Criminal Action Papers, 1760–71; *Crown v. White* and *Crown v. Rogers*, March, 1746, General Court Criminal Papers—General and Assize Courts, 1745–49; *Crown v. Hutchins* and *Crown v. Downs*, March, 1762, *Crown v. Nicholas* and *Crown v. Henricks*, January, 1764, Salisbury District Court Criminal Action Papers, 1760–71; *Crown v. Allen*, October, 1731, July, 1732, etc., General Court Criminal Papers, 1730–34; *Crown v. Young*, July, 1736, General Court Criminal Papers, 1735–37; *Crown v. Sanders*, March, 1745, General Court Criminal Papers—General and Assize Courts, 1745–49, and General Court Dockets, 1745–46; *Crown v. Lee*, September, 1758, Tyrrell County Court Minutes, 1735–61.

selling liquor to slaves, sailors, or servants without their masters' permission. In 1741 the assembly provided special legislation, the "Regulation of Ordinaries, and other Houses of Entertainment." Taverns created fertile ground for misbehavior. Widow Elizabeth Marston, keeper of a tavern in Edenton in the 1720s and allegedly "a common Bawd," allowed "the persons that frequent her house" to commit "great disorders to the disturbance and annoyance . . . of the neighborhood." In 1736 the General Court indicted Mary and William Waltham for entertaining thieves and robbers at their ordinary, and for engaging in theft themselves as well. Another couple, Margaret and Robert Kingham, allegedly ran an unlicensed "tippling house." Other indictments against them included assault, theft, murder, and escape from jail.[13]

Ordinaries sometimes provided a setting for a common morals offense—blasphemy. In prosecuting men and women who took God's name in vain, the criminal courts underscored the intimate link between law and morality. John Hassell earned thirty-nine lashes in 1722 for announcing after a sermon one Sunday that "If an Angell should come down from Heaven and tell him face to face that he should Dye and be Damned to all Eternity he would not forbear Swearing at Some times." A more fortunate William Hamilton was acquitted in 1744 for claiming that "throwing a Little cold water on Infants would do as much good as Baptism . . . and that the Bible . . . contained a heap of Lyes." Mary Silva's blasphemous speech led her to be "Carted about town with labells on her back."[14]

Buggery was so serious and heinous an offense against morality that it was treated as a felony. Only a few cases appear in the records. In 1764 a higher court accused John Everitt, laborer, of having "a venereal affair with . . . a Mare." Robert Johnson, hatter, allegedly "did commit and perpetrate that detestable and abominable Crime of buggery (not to be named among Christians)" with a black cow.[15] Although these illustrations are rare, their very appearance in the records points to a link

13. Act of 1715, *NCSR*, XXIII, 3–6; act of 1741, *ibid.*, 173–74, 182–85; Marston court order, January 17, 1725, General Court Criminal Papers, 1720–29; *Marston v. Havett*, July, 1725, *NCHCR*, VI, 128; *Crown v. Walthams*, March, 1736, General Court Criminal Papers, 1735–37; *Crown v. Kinghams*, March, 1733, July, 1735, March, 1736, *NCSR*, II, 553–54, and General Court Criminal Papers, 1730–34, 1735–37.

14. *Crown v. Hassell*, March, 1722, *NCHCR*, V, 202, 210, 214, 225–26, 241, 289; *Crown v. Hamilton*, October, 1744, General Court Dockets, 1744, and General Court Criminal Papers, 1740–44; *Crown v. Silva*, March, 1765, Salisbury District Court Trial and Minute Docket, 1761–90.

15. *Crown v. Everitt*, May, 1764, Edenton District Court Records, 1765; *Crown v. Johnson*, September, 1765, Salisbury District Court Criminal Action Papers, 1760–71.

between moral behavior and social control. This kind of sexual deviancy, whether suspected or actually proved, went so beyond the norm that it posed a grave threat to the natural order.

Most moral misbehavior is clearly defined in the records, but clerks used the word *trespass* to describe a number of different offenses for which definitions are rare. Trespass was originally a criminal action at common law. By the eighteenth century, it was more usually a civil action to recover damages to person or property. Hawkins defined trespasses as "all inferior Offenses, which are properly and directly against the Peace, and Assaults and Batteries." These actions must "have a direct and immediate Tendency to cause such Breaches of the Peace." Jacob's *Law Dictionary*, a reference text of the Carolina courts, called trespass more precisely a wrong "done by one private Man to another . . . with Force." In colonies such as New York and Virginia, trespass was usually a civil action, nor did it appear often as a criminal action in the records of seventeenth-century colonial courts.[16] But in North Carolina, for reasons not apparent in the records, clerks often recorded different kinds of criminal acts as trespass. In 1726, for example, the General Court grand jury indicted George Burrington "for Trespass assault Misdemeanor and breach of the peace." William McKinnie's trespass, of which he was acquitted by the New Bern District Court in 1759, was noted a felony. In 1764 the Salisbury District Court convicted Daniel Harmon of a trespass recorded as animal stealing.[17] But most often the clerk left no clue to what, exactly, constituted a trespass. It may have been assault, theft, contempt, but most likely the offense was accompanied by force or the intent to use it. Without statutory guides, the Carolina courts apparently prosecuted some forms of trespass as public wrongs.

Offenses against public order—riot, affray, forcible entry, breach of peace, and libel—could be felonies or lesser crimes, depending on their "degree of malignity." In one way or another, all had the effect of disturbing the public peace. An affray, for example, which involved the

16. Hawkins, *A Treatise of the Pleas of the Crown*, II, 40; Cynthia B. Herrup, *The Common Peace: Participation and the Criminal Law in Seventeenth-Century England* (Cambridge, England, 1987), 3; Jacob, *Law Dictionary;* Goebel and Naughton, *Law Enforcement in Colonial New York*; Hoffer and Scott (eds.), *Criminal Proceedings in Colonial Virginia*, lv; Chapin, *Criminal Justice in Colonial America*.

17. *Crown v. Burrington*, March, 1726, NCHCR, VI, 225; *Crown v. McKinnie*, September, 1759, New Bern District Court Trial, Argument, Reference, and Appearance Docket, 1758–60; *Crown v. Harmon*, September, 1764, Salisbury District Court Trial and Minute Docket, 1761–90.

"Fighting of Two or More to the Terror of the King's Subjects," violated the public peace, whereas an assault, which was fighting in private, did not.[18] A libel, which exposed a person to contempt and ridicule, could threaten the peace by provoking the victim "to revenge, and perhaps to bloodshed." Riots, or the assembly of "Three or more Persons" who attempt to carry out an unlawful act "with Force," were the most common of the offenses against public order.[19] While the circumstances of each episode are rarely revealed, the context and the participants can sometimes overcome that silence. At the Salisbury District Court, in September, 1765, no fewer than fifty men were indicted for riot and then discharged at the next court session. These men were involved in the violent uprising over land problems that had broken out in the western counties of Anson and Mecklenburg the previous spring.[20]

Assaults, thefts, murders, immorality, so common in the Carolina world, are the acts of real people challenging the society's norms of godliness, decency, and behavior. North Carolinians also committed at least twenty-nine other felonies and misdemeanors that, taken together, offer an insight into the rhythms of eighteenth-century life. Counterfeiting, forgery, sedition, arson, and fraud occurred, as did a large number of irksome acts called "nuisance": allowing animals to roam, failing to repair roads and fences, creating a fire hazard. Men and women convicted of cheat or deceit had sold defective goods or altered official papers. Now and then the records point to an unusual action that went against the grain and was therefore cognizable at common law. The General Court grand jury in 1715 presented John Wattson for selling "Five barrels of Pitch as good and merchantable Pitch" that "was found and adjudged to be not good Pitch." John Twanbrook allegedly caused a fire danger in 1736 by building a pine chimney in his house. In 1741 the Carteret County court acquitted George Bell, Sr., of detaining and abusing an orphan. The General Court in 1745 accused John Hill, esquire, of placing a barrel of salt among fifteen filled with pork. And in 1766 a grand jury dismissed a charge against butcher John Beard for selling spoiled meat. The records also show three charges of forestalling, fourteen of selling liquor without a license, and two grand jury presentments

18. Blackstone, *Commentaries*, IV, 142; Wood, *An Institute*, IV, 425.
19. Blackstone, *Commentaries*, IV, 150; Davis, *Justice of Peace*, 295.
20. For riot indictments, see September, 1765, and March, 1766, in Salisbury District Court Trial and Minute Docket, 1761–90. On land riots, see A. Roger Ekirch, "North Carolina Regulators on Liberty and Corruption," *Perspectives in American History*, XI (1977–78), 220–22; and Lefler and Powell, *Colonial North Carolina*, 229.

of Susannah Evans and Martha Richardson for "Diabolically and ma-
litiously bewitch[ing] several . . . of her Majesties Liege subjects."[21]

Given the presence of slaves in the colony from a very early time,
North Carolina had to develop, as did other slave societies, new definitions for the crimes of blacks. White law, and all that it implied about the
nature of man, was simply not relevant to slaves. In and of itself, slave
crime reflected a kind of behavior for which there was little counterpart
in the white world. Black criminals, for example, generally posed a
threat not to the order of their own community but to that of their white
masters. Slaves who committed crimes may have tried, just as lower-
crust whites and servants did, to better their own circumstances. But
they were motivated as well by the desire to challenge their oppression,
to exercise some control over a life of near absolute compliance. In this
way slave crime was in fact a form of resistance.[22] The truly odious
circumstances that led to slave crime, and the colony's special way of
handling it, make description virtually impossible without a fair
amount of speculation.[23] Records of lesser crimes basically do not exist,
for masters dealt with these actions summarily. Before 1715, slaves
accused of serious offenses were tried in the highest court along with
freemen. A very early case is that of "A Negroe boy named Exeter," tried
by the County Court jury in 1687 for the murder of his master. In 1698,
"One Negro of the said Capt. Anthony Dawson" joined with Dawson
and several freemen to strip and destroy a shipwreck. A trial jury found
"the said Negroe . . . guilty of firing the Gun." The circumstances surrounding Elizabeth Baker's murder in 1699 can only be imagined, but a
General Court jury heard "A Negro Slave belonging to Mr. Thomas
Vandermulen" confess to the crime.[24]

21. Goebel and Naughton, *Law Enforcement in Colonial New York*, 98; *Crown v. Wattson*, October, 1715, NCHCR, V, 85; *Crown v. Twanbrook*, November, 1736, General Court Criminal Papers, 1735–37; *Crown v. Bell*, June, 1741, Carteret County Court
Dockets, 1731–62; *Crown v. Hill*, March, 1745, General Court Criminal Papers—General and Assize Courts, 1745–49; *Crown v. Beard*, Salisbury District Court Criminal
Action Papers, 1760–71. On bewitching, see *NCHCR*, IV, 65–72.

22. See Marvin L. Michael Kay and Lorin Lee Cary, " 'They are Indeed the Constant
Plague of Their Tryants': Slave Defence of a Moral Economy in Colonial North Carolina,
1748–1772," *Slavery and Abolition*, VI (1985), 37–56.

23. Kay and Cary, who have done excellent work on slave crime in North Carolina,
confront the paucity of records when they refer to "a too limited sample," "the few extant
records," and "the small sample" (*ibid.*, 40–43).

24. *Proprietors v. Exeter*, December, 1687, *NCHCR*, II, 378; *Crown v. Dawson et al.*,
May, 1698, *Crown v. Peter*, March, 1699, *NCHCR*, III, 216–17, 262.

Records of the slave tribunals created by statute in 1715 to deal with serious slave crime are quite sparse in comparison to the data generated by the regular courts. One study of the years 1755 to 1770 found that slaveowners sought public reimbursement for 59 slaves executed for crimes. Nearly one-quarter were charged with murder or attempted murder. The victims were typically white. A parallel investigation, for the years 1748 to 1772, found that 115 slaves had been either executed or castrated. Their crimes included murder and assault (44 percent), theft (26 percent), runaway or outlaw (21 percent), rape (6 percent), and arson (3 percent). Perhaps the most important category of slave crime was running away. This particular offense, committed by slaves who "stole themselves," most assuredly troubled the white population greatly. Legislators constantly tinkered with slave codes to discourage runaways. By piecing together data from scattered newspapers and advertisements, Kay and Cary find evidence of 134 runaways between 1748 and 1775, a figure that probably does not come close to the actual number.[25] Whatever the motive—permanent freedom, a respite from toil, a family visit—a slave fleeing bondage carried out the ultimate act of resistance. Herein a slave could most effectively break down a system that sustained his or her own oppression. Given the difficulty of succeeding, the act itself of running away had greater emotional importance than did the potentially horrendous outcome.

The overwhelming evidence of criminal activity in North Carolina relates to the actions of whites. During the colonial period, eight major categories of crime demanded the attention of the Carolina courts (Table 2). Even a quick glance at the figures, with assault composing nearly one-third of all prosecutions, establishes North Carolina as an unruly colony, particularly when lower assault rates prevailed in New York and Massachusetts.[26] Assault was the most frequently prosecuted offense in North Carolina, and that was true in every decade after 1730 (Table 3). Nor did personal violence occur most often in any one region (Table 4). Demographic change indicates too that assault was an ever-present and

25. Alan D. Watson, "Impulse Toward Independence; Resistance and Rebellion Among North Carolina Slaves, 1750–1775," *Journal of Negro History,* LXIII (1978), 319–20; Kay and Cary, " 'They are Indeed the Constant Plague,' " 49, 39–41; Marvin L. Michael Kay and Lorin Lee Cary, "Slave Runaways in Colonial North Carolina, 1748–1775," *NCHR,* LXIII (1986), 1–39.

26. Greenberg, *Crime and Law Enforcement in New York,* 50; Edwin Powers, *Crime and Punishment in Early Massachusetts, 1620–1692: a documentary history* (Boston, 1966), 404–407, 451.

TABLE 2
CRIMINAL ACTIONS, 1670–1776

Crime	Number	Percentage of All Prosecutions
Assault	1,299	31.62
Theft	522	12.70
Crimes against morality	340	8.27
Trespass	246	5.98
Animal stealing	217	5.28
Contempt	145	3.53
Crimes against public order	130	3.16
Homicide	111	2.70
Other[1]	1,098	26.72
Total	4,108	99.96

[1]Includes 29 different offenses (472 total charges) plus an additional 626 charges that are not identifiable in the records.

TABLE 3
CRIMINAL ACTIONS, BY DECADE, 1720–1769

| | | | | | | Percentage Prosecuted | | | | |
Decade	Number	Assault	Theft	Morals Crimes	Trespass	Contempt	Animal Stealing	Crimes Against Order	Homicide	Other
1720s	166	4.22%	19.28%	19.87%	—	13.86%	1.20%	3.61%	9.64%	28.31%
1730s	349	26.65	19.77	7.16	2.58%	8.02	4.58	4.58	6.02	20.62
1740s	489	28.04	13.20	12.16	6.60	3.30	5.57	1.85	3.09	26.19
1750s	609	38.51	9.27	6.12	6.79	2.81	2.29	2.15	1.82	30.13
1760s	1,521	35.25	11.68	6.27	4.55	2.44	5.68	4.95	1.91	27.26

TABLE 4
CRIMINAL ACTIONS, BY REGION, 1663–1776

Region	Number	Assault	Theft	Morals Crimes	Trespass	Contempt	Animal Stealing	Crimes Against Order	Homicide	Other
Albemarle	1,155	33.24%	14.28%	9.17%	6.49%	4.58%	6.06%	0.95%	2.25%	22.94%
South central	523	41.10	11.28	7.07	2.67	1.33	2.86	2.48	2.10	29.06
East central	654	45.71	8.71	6.42	3.97	2.14	2.14	2.14	1.68	27.06
North central	241	21.99	8.29	19.50	5.39	1.24	1.24	0.82	0.82	40.66
West	911	24.91	13.40	4.50	9.22	3.18	9.65	7.13	2.63	25.24
Total	3,484									

Percentage Prosecuted

Albemarle counties: Bertie, Chowan, Currituck, Hertford, Pasquotank, Perquimans, Tyrrell

South central counties: Bladen, Brunswick, Cumberland, Duplin, New Hanover, Onslow

East central counties: Bath, Beaufort, Carteret, Craven, Dobbs, Hyde, Pitt

North central counties: Bute, Chatham, Edgecombe, Granville, Halifax, Johnston, Northampton, Wake

Western counties: Anson, Guilford, Mecklenburg, Orange, Rowan, Surry, Tryon

ever-growing challenge to stability. Between 1735 and 1760, when the white population doubled, assault prosecutions tripled.[27] Even contemporary accounts seem to focus on disorder, especially in the early years. When the colony was still sparsely settled in 1700, Edmund Randolph lamented the lack of "settled Government." Eighteen years later, John Urmston, a missionary who spent an unpleasant decade in the colony, noted bitterly in a letter home that "the spirit of contradiction reigns here, they are not to be governed, but by methods of their own contriving." Nor did this "independent" style of living seem to improve over time. During the politically turbulent 1720s, Attorney General William Little, embroiled in the discord himself, observed that "the Authority of Government has been suffered to sink so low & the Courts so much obstructed that Law & Justice seemed at a stand." Thirty years later, a North Carolina traveler found the backcountry to be "a Stage of Debauchery Dissoluteness and Corruption." These conditions were apparently responsible for a vagrancy act passed in 1755. It prescribed close regulation and severe punishment for those living an "idle and disorderly Life."[28]

To be sure, there is a risk in emphasizing the large proportion of assault charges in the records, since there is no necessary connection between any criminal charge and actual behavior. At the same time, the high rate of assault prosecutions creates the unavoidable impression of a society troubled by personal violence. Was North Carolina, in fact, an unruly place? Or is there a different story to be told? Assault was, after all, a relatively easy crime to prosecute. When victims knew their attackers, evidence was not hard to collect. Yet in a puzzling sort of way, colonists continued to come to blows at a steadily increasing rate as the eighteenth century advanced. Perhaps a maturing colony was reacting to disorder. Or perhaps the colony's relative safety from Indian attacks created an atmosphere more conducive to personal violence. Yet the

27. Population in 1735 was 40,000; in 1760 it was 80,000. Assaults in 1735 totaled 11, or 34.4 percent of all prosecutions; assaults in 1760 totaled 41, or 48.6 percent of all prosecutions. Put another way, assault charges were made at a rate of 27.5/100,000 in 1735, and the rate was 42.5/100,000 in 1760. For population figures, see Evarts B. Greene and Virginia D. Harrington, *American Population Before the Federal Census of 1790* (New York, 1932), 157–58.

28. Edmund Randolph to [?], March 24, 1700, in *NCSR*, I, 527; John Urmston to Society for the Propagation of the Gospel, October 18, 1718, in *NCSR*, II, 310; William Little to [?], August, 1731, in *NCSR*, III, 200; Charles Woodmason, *The Carolina Backcountry on the Eve of the Revolution*, ed. Richard J. Hooker (Chapel Hill, 1953), 80–81; act of 1755, *NCSR*, XXIII, 435.

most compelling explanation may lie in North Carolina's unusually diverse religions. "Every sect of religion abounds here except the Roman Catholic," wrote Governor Tryon in 1765. "No British colony on this continent stands in more, or so much need of regular moral clergymen, as this does," he complained.[29] North Carolina lacked the spiritual restraint that prevailed in, say, Anglican Virginia or Congregational New England. Indeed, there was no dominant church to sustain a certain amount of social cohesion.

Perhaps the most oft cited comment on the early period of Carolina history was by Thomas Lowndes, who caustically called the province "a Receptacle for Pyrates Thieves and Vagabonds of all sorts." Indeed, prosecutions for theft in the colony occurred at a relatively high rate. Lowndes's observation, however, is still misleading, for property crimes were also quite common in eighteenth-century England, early New York, and Massachusetts.[30] What is of interest about North Carolina is that the colony failed to sustain the same large number of theft prosecutions relative to all others (see Table 3). In 1725, there were seven theft charges per ten thousand persons; in 1748, there were three; in 1765, there was one; and in 1770, there was one.[31] That decline can be explained in a number of ways. More effective law enforcement in later years may have discouraged stealing. Or, as the economy became increasingly complex, other kinds of criminal acts became more attractive. And the middle-class character of North Carolina, the widespread landholding and comfortable if not meager existence of many whites, might have diminished the pool of potential thieves.

Recent studies of slave crime conclude that bondspeople engaged in a substantial number of offenses against property.[32] Even as early as

29. Ekirch, "*Poor Carolina*," 217–18; Tyron to Society for the Propagation of the Gospel, July 31, 1765, in *NCSR*, VII, 102–103.

30. Thomas Lowndes to Board of Trade, December 8, 1729, in *NCSR*, III, 49; J. S. Cockburn, "The Nature and Incidence of Crime in England 1559–1625: A Preliminary Survey," in Cockburn (ed.), *Crime in England*, 55; Beattie, "Crime and the Courts in Surrey," in Cockburn (ed.), *Crime in England*, 155; Greenberg, *Crime and Law Enforcement in New York*, 50; Powers, *Crime and Punishment in Early Massachusetts*, 404–408.

31. White population figures are followed by theft charges: 10,000/7 in 1725; 14,689/5 in 1748; 120,519/13 in 1765; 152,250/16 in 1770. Throughout this study, population figures include whites only (unless noted otherwise) and are compiled from Greene and Harrington, *American Population*, following the procedure described in Merrens, *Colonial North Carolina in the Eighteenth Century*, 195–98.

32. Kay and Cary, " 'They are Indeed the Constant Plague,' " 49. Also see Crow, *The Black Experience in Revolutionary North Carolina*, Chap. 3.

1685, the County Court convicted and banished Mingo, a slave, "for Running away from the house of Daniell Akehurst Esqr. and Carrying away severall goods belonging to him." Nearly a century later, Janet Schaw noted as she traveled through the colony that slaves "steal whatever they can come at." Increasingly harsh slave codes and local laws to prevent trading between blacks and whites made clear the difficulty of controlling slaves' crimes against property. A law in 1741, for example, prohibited whites, servant or free, from trading with slaves. While slaves probably stole from each other as well as from whites, they did so to better their circumstances, no matter how temporary the improvement, or to rebel against a system that took everything from them and gave them nothing in return. Stephen, along with a slave accomplice named Jack, broke out of jail in late November, 1748, and went on a rampage. In the course of a night, the two men "stole three bottles of Rum, . . . a watch . . . one worsted Mittan, one Snuff box and Sundry small articles." They had seized the items from a store owned by Charles Simpson after breaking down the "door with a Chisel and Tomahawk." In 1765 a freeholders court held in Tarboro looked into a charge against Jamey, "a certain Negro Slave the Property of a Person unknown for Robbery." No doubt hoping to sell the goods, Jamey broke into a house and stole a lot of items, including "one Coat Jacket & Breeches one Rifle Gun one Womans Scarlet Cloak 1 printed Linnen Handkerchief." Nearly ten years later, another male slave, London, faced a freeholders court in Halifax County that, after hearing "Sundry Witnesses," found London guilty of stealing "a certain Sum of Money" on at least three occasions.[33]

One of the most vexing and probably easiest forms of theft was animal stealing. Year after year the records contain accounts of lost or mismarked cattle, pigs, and horses. Animal stealing was one of the few offenses cited in the colony's public papers as a growing cause for alarm. In 1741 the assembly directed new and harsher legislation to the "many Wicked Men . . . , being too lazy to get their Living by honest Labour, [who] make it their Business to ride in the Woods and steal Cattle and Hogs." Slaves added considerably to the problem of keeping livestock

33. *Proprietors v. Mingo*, November, 1685, NCHCR, II, 364; Janet Schaw, *Journal of a Lady of Quality*, ed. Evangeline W. Andrews and Charles M. Andrews (New Haven, 1923), 177; act of 1741, NCSR, XXIII, 194; *Crown v. Stephen*, December, 1748, Secretary of State, Court Records, Magistrates and Freeholders Courts; *Crown v. Jamey*, April, 1765, and *Crown v. London*, May, 1774, Halifax District Court Miscellaneous Records, 1763–1808.

secure, especially runaways who "lie out hid and lurking in the Swamps, Woods and other Obscure Places, killing Cattle and Hogs." In 1741 the assembly prohibited bondsmen from raising livestock for their own use and provided gruesome punishments for slaves who stole or killed animals. Cato, for example, was an accused hog thief. He "was Grinding at the Mill" when he threw an ax at a hog and killed it. Cato denied that he knew the animal belonged to his mistress. For this offense, he was whipped and lost his ears.[34]

Given the high value of horses, and the relatively easy task of stealing them (enclosures were rare), horse thieves apparently were quite common in the colony. One observer noted with some concern in 1752 that "Bands of horse thieves have been infesting portions of the State & pursuing their nefarious calling a long time." Four members of the Sparkmen gang in Tyrrell County faced several separate indictments during the 1760s for stealing horses. And in 1775, Joseph Pittoway, a horse thief and "pest of Society . . . made his exit at the Gallows." These thefts, so difficult to control, led Governor Tryon to issue a proclamation in 1767 calling "for the apprehending and bringing to Justice certain Gangs of Horse Stealers and Rogues." In 1771, there were four men who apparently terrorized the people of Wilmington by horse stealing "and other offences." They sat in the town jail, awaiting trial.[35]

While assault and theft demanded many work hours from Carolina lawmen, so did a set of offenses that in a modern context would not be crimes at all. Morals prosecutions were common in all colonies, though the Carolina data do not mirror the high rate tabulated for Massachusetts.[36] The incidence of one offense—bastardy—is not accurately reflected in the records, since bastardy proceedings, unless initiated by a

34. Act of 1741, *NCSR*, XXIII, 165–201; *Crown v. Cato*, February, 1748, Miscellaneous Collections, Slavery Papers, 1747–1850.

35. Diary of Bishop Spangenburg, September 12, 1752, in *NCSR*, IV, 1312; Tyrrell County Court Prosecution, Reference, and New Action Dockets, 1756–85, Edenton District Court Crown Docket Superior Court, May, 1765–October, 1769, Edenton District Court Criminal Action Papers, 1756–1806; *North Carolina Gazette*, July 14, 1775; Proclamation, July 16, 1767, *NCSR*, VII, 503–504; council meeting, January 12, 1771, *NCSR*, VIII, 481, and *Crown v. Hues*, February, 1771, Wilmington District Court Minutes, Superior Court, 1760–83.

36. Powers, *Crime and Punishment in Early Massachusetts*, 404–407; David Flaherty, "Law and the Enforcement of Morals in Early America," in Lawrence Friedman and Harry Scheiber (eds.), *American Law and the Constitutional Order* (Cambridge, Mass., 1978), 53–66.

presentment or challenged by a named father, were conducted by magistrates out of court. Surviving records reveal the unlikely total of forty-six bastardy prosecutions for the entire colonial period, with no more than six in any given year. However many morals prosecutions there may actually have been, North Carolina was certainly no den of iniquity. Just as other colonies showed a declining interest in treating sin as a crime, so did this province. In fact, North Carolina's interest declined in a far more significant way. During the 1750s, county courts in Connecticut and Massachusetts were devoting 25 and 60 percent of their business, respectively, to morals prosecutions. The same charges amounted to only 10 percent in the Carolina courts.[37] Immoral behavior also diminished in importance relative to other transgressions. Consider that in the 1740s the courts prosecuted 1.08 thefts for every morals offense, in the 1750s the figure was 1.1 and in the 1760s it was 1.9. Perhaps North Carolinians showed comparatively less concern for moral misbehavior because ordinary acts of swearing, drunkenness, and adultery did not occur often enough to trouble them. Yet a contemporary reference to the backcountry as an "*Augean* Stable" where "Polygamy is very Common—Celibacy much more—Bastardy, no Disrepute—Concubinage General" lends little support to this assessment. Indeed, contemporary remarks on the colonists' improving morality are exceedingly rare. Once again, the religious environment, or lack of it, offers the best explanation for North Carolina's secularization. Governor Johnston agreed with other observers in 1736 when he complained to the assembly about "the deplorable & almost totall want of divine worship throughout the Province." This apparent indifference to religion accounts, at least in part, for the declining interest in prosecuting morals offenses. Perhaps the most compelling explanation has to do with the growth of the colony itself. Dramatic demographic change and urban growth generated a whole new range of offenses, some quite serious. Moral misbehavior seemed less threatening and, when compared to property crime, did not seem worth pursuing.[38]

The fluctuation of contempt prosecutions, while similar to those in

37. Flaherty, "Law and the Enforcement of Morals," 61; Hoffer and Scott (eds.), *Criminal Proceedings in Colonial Virginia*, xxvii; Greenberg, "Crime, Law Enforcement, and Social Control," 305.

38. Woodmason, *The Carolina Backcountry*, 81; Address of Governor Johnston, September 22, 1736, *NCSR*, IV 227; Flaherty, "Law and the Enforcement of Morals," 59–65.

New York, gives special insight into North Carolina's own peculiar circumstances.[39] The bulk of the charges are grouped in the 1720s and 1730s, after which the proportion of contempt prosecutions in the records steadily declined. Some of the charges in the early period were spawned, no doubt, by the political chaos recounted so often in histories of the colony. Edmund Porter, a prominent opponent of Governor Richard Everard, was indicted by the General Court grand jury in 1727 for threatening "to raise force against the Government in great contempt of Authority" and for insulting the governor "with his hatt on with a menacing Countenance." The next year a grand jury indicted John Lovick, secretary of the colony, for giving Everard "ill language and Blows."[40] While these prosecutions highlight the political infighting in the 1720s, the vast majority of contempt charges resulted not from political strife but from ordinary acts disrespectful of government and the law. Indeed, these findings agree with studies that note the troubled history of early North Carolina. During that rough-and-tumble period of transition from proprietary to royal control, colonists attacked tax collectors, verbally and physically abused lawmen, and resisted arrest. Contempt charges never disappeared from the records, but they became much less important with the passage of time. As the colony matured, law enforcers clearly commanded greater respect from the people or had the means to control them more effectively.

Were the people of any particular region in the colony more inclined to resist authority? The differences in rates of prosecution for contempt are not highly significant (Table 4). Since Albemarle included some of the oldest counties in the colony, the political turmoil that occurred there in the early period explains the overall large proportion of its contempt charges. The experience of the western counties is likewise predictable. During the 1760s—the most turbulent period of the Regulation—73 percent of the total number of contempt actions occurred in the west.[41] The western region also provided a setting for a large proportion of all crimes against public order. County courts there generated nearly 70 percent of riot charges recorded across the entire colonial

39. The rate of prosecution for contempt cases in New York was 5.9 percent. See Greenberg, *Crime and Law Enforcement in New York*, 50.

40. *Crown v. Porter*, March, 1727, and *Crown v. Lovick*, October, 1728, NCHCR, VI, 369–70, 535.

41. There were thirty-seven contempt prosecutions overall in the 1760s, and twenty-seven of them occurred in the western counties.

period. All but two of these charges occurred at the height of the Regulation. Disorder may have been pervasive in the western counties during the 1760s, but evidence from the records also stresses that this was an isolated phenomenon, that disorder did not permeate the Carolina world at other times, except for the 1720s.

The broad prosecution patterns for antigovernment crimes add some detail to the standard portrayal of North Carolina as a lawless place.[42] Together, these offenses represented less than 8 percent of all criminal charges. Civil strife, it seems clear, seldom escalated into serious resistance to authority. Violent behavior certainly brought colonists into court at a higher rate than did any other offense, but assaults were sparked by the kind of personal discord that had little or nothing to do with government.

The last major category of criminal prosecutions is homicide, a difficult crime to assess since comparative data are scarce. Like colonists elsewhere, North Carolinians killed their friends, spouses, children, and slaves. But they did this in declining proportions relative to other crimes as time passed. And the number of murders decidedly fell while the population increased. In 1721, murder prosecutions occurred at a rate of 7 per 10,000 persons; in 1735, at 1 per 10,000; in 1755, at 1.7 per 10,000; and in 1765, at .66 per 10,000.[43] Fewer murders reflected a more stable and orderly world in which grievances rarely led to death. Perhaps authoritarian institutions simply had more effective control.

Slave murderers fall into a category all their own because their victims were usually white. In 1768 a Northampton County freeholders court convicted Robin, Jamey, and Jack, on their own confession, of the murder of their master, Samuel Thomas. The same year, Ned, a slave, was the defendant in two murder trials. First, a Bute County court considered a charge against him for "Poisoning a Negro Slave named Jemmie" and found him "not Guilty of the Crime laid to his Charge in such a degree as to be punishable with death." Ned was again in court less than two months later, this time convicted of poisoning William Williamson, the master of his accomplice. Eight justices attended this trial rather than the usual three or four, and given the nature of the

42. See, for example, Richard M. Brown, "Violence and the American Revolution," in Stephen G. Kurtz and James H. Hutson (eds.), *Essays on the American Revolution* (Chapel Hill, 1973), 86, 94–95; Ekirch, "*Poor Carolina*," 215–16.
43. White population figures are followed by homicide charges. 4,200/3 in 1721; 40,000/5 in 1735; 50,000/3 in 1755; 120,519/8 in 1765.

charge, this is not surprising. In 1769, Will, planning to murder a white woman, killed himself when the plot was discovered. And Rose, convicted of arson and attempted murder, had apparently told a witness that "the next time She Run away, she would burn some of their Houses over their heads."[44] Slaves who murdered whites certainly represented the ultimate and most terrifying challenge to bondage, and they were dealt with accordingly.

The broad changes in kind and number of criminal prosecutions were tied precisely to those elusive factors that have an impact on crime patterns in any era: actual increases in or new definitions of criminal behavior, better ways of reporting crime, shifts in the desire or ability of officials or the people to enforce the law, and economic and demographic change. Given the nature of crime and its causes, precise analyses are simply not possible. But by dissecting the data into ten-year periods, which are admittedly artificial categories, we can uncover some significant configurations in the Carolina world. Even as early as 1700 through 1719, it is easy to see that the courts were busy with prosecutions for immorality, assault, animal stealing, and theft. All these offenses were major ones in later years. Prosecution patterns for the 1720s accurately reflect the political contours of the time, for antigovernment offenses figured more importantly than they did in any other period. Contempt and sedition composed 20.5 percent of all charges recorded for the 1720s. Even more telling are the sedition charges alone. Eleven accusations of sedition came before the courts during this ten-year period, nearly half of all such actions recorded in the colony's history. No evidence more clearly points to the chaotic state of provincial politics.[45]

The troubles in the 1720s visibly spilled over into the next decade. In 1729, Governor Everard suspended the chief justice, causing "a great defect of Justice & delay in business."[46] The Crown decided in the same year to end ineffective proprietary rule in the colony and to appoint the controversial George Burrington as the first royal governor. A dramatic drop in criminal actions, in 1729 and 1730, coincided with these events.

44. *Crown v. Robin, Jamey, and Jack,* March, 1768, Halifax District Superior Court Miscellaneous Records, 1758–1806: *Crown v. Ned,* March, 1768, Bute County Court Minutes, 1767–76; *Crown v. Ned and Daniel,* May, 1768, Secretary of State, Court Records, Magistrates and Freeholders Courts; Deposition of T. Hall, August, 1769, *ibid.*; *Crown v. Rose,* n.d., Halifax District Superior Court Miscellaneous Records, 1763–1808.
    45. There were twenty-four sedition charges during the entire colonial period.
    46. William Badham to George Burrington, August 2, 1731, in *NCSR,* III, 198.

Burrington's arrival in the colony, along with the appointment of a new chief justice, led the courts to resume their former activity, though political strife was still the order of the day. The appointment of Gabriel Johnston in 1734, whose long administration brought periodic stability to the colony, did not immediately end the general lawlessness evident in the criminal court records. A growing number of prosecutions for assault hinted that personal violence would increase as the colony developed. The simple fact, too, that the courts handled more than twice as many criminal actions in the 1730s as in the previous decade suggests a maturing of legal institutions and their growing effectiveness.

The 1740s heralded some dramatic changes in the aftermath of the court law of 1738. Almost immediately, the county courts were involved in more criminal actions. In the 1720s and 1730s, they prosecuted only 5 percent and then 15 percent of all cases. By the 1750s, they were busy with more than half. While the county courts never undertook the bulk of criminal business handled by lower courts in Virginia, they did, beginning in the 1740s, assume authority previously exercised by the General Court.[47] In the 1730s, for example, the lower courts acted on only 3 percent of all theft charges, a figure that jumped to 15.6 percent in the next decade. Assault proceedings in those courts leaped from 9.7 percent in the 1730s to 24 percent roughly ten years later. By far the most important outcome of the court law was that justices of the peace could play a more potent role in provincial concerns. When the criminal authority of the county courts expanded, so did the power of local judges. Now the day-to-day criminality of North Carolinians would be handled much closer to the site where it occurred. Community members would have more to do with regulating behavior. And justices of the peace, already prominent socially and politically could use their increased criminal authority at home to elevate their role in the larger colony as well.

Evidence from the records of the 1740s also shows that the colony, at least for a time, was enjoying the stability that had proved elusive in earlier years. Contempt and sedition charges were clearly on the decline. The proportion of theft charges also decreased. This could mean that fewer thefts occurred or that colonists were engaging in a wide variety of crimes. The colony's dramatic physical growth could also account for that decline. Sparsely settled areas offer little worth stealing and make it

---

47. Hoffer and Scott (eds.), *Criminal Proceedings in Colonial Virginia*, xvii–xviii.

difficult for lawmen to prosecute thieves. Toward the end of the 1740s, bitter political battles once again disrupted the courts as northerners and southerners debated the issue of representation in the assembly. Criminal court actions declined dramatically. The Moravian bishop August Spangenburg wrote an oft-quoted lament: "The Counties are in conflict with one another," weakening the authority "of the magistrates." In the northeast "a perfect anarchy" prevailed. "As a result, crimes are of frequent occurrence, such as murder robbery &c. But the criminals cannot be brought to justice."[48] Spangenburg was correct. Until the political dust had settled, the courts prosecuted a trivial number of assaults and thefts.

Not until 1753 did the criminal courts begin to resume their previous duties. By then, Arthur Dobbs had succeeded Johnston as governor, and northern and southern counties were patching up their differences. For the courts and the colony itself, the 1750s were an important period of transition. The general and assize courts gave way, briefly, to five new supreme courts, and the change, while mostly one of form, caused some visible interruption in legal proceedings. Despite impressive population growth, both slave and free, the courts did not process the number of criminal actions that we might expect. Nor does the evidence on serious slave crime show much activity in the 1750s.[49] If the data for the 1750s are remarkable in any way, it is because of the very large proportion of assault charges, larger than for any other ten-year period. Rapid demographic change may have created an atmosphere conducive to personal violence. Since half of all assault actions with a known location (105 of 207 charges) were generated in the east central region, population density could explain the comparatively high level of personal violence there.

What stands out about the 1760s is that the courts prosecuted two and one half times as many criminal actions as they had in the previous decade. Population growth, the addition of new counties, and the creation of another judicial district, all help explain that tremendous increase. Evidence from the records of the 1760s also shows that, remarkably, the courts prosecuted 41 percent of all assaults for the colonial period in this decade. Did Regulator unrest contribute to a climate of personal violence in the west? The evidence says no. During the 1760s, assaults composed 26 percent of all prosecutions in the western coun-

48. Diary of Bishop Spangenburg, September 12, 1752, in NCSR, IV, 1311–12.
49. Kay and Cary, " 'They are Indeed the Constant Plague,' " 50.

ties. However, the figure was 50 percent in the east central counties and 38 percent in the Albemarle counties.

In the final six years of the colonial period, as the higher court system collapsed, the number of criminal actions handled by the courts declined dramatically and predictably. In fact, the county courts conducted most of the criminal prosecutions (71 percent). During these last years before the Revolution, colonists apparently engaged in the same kinds of misbehavior that had always brought them into court.

An essential point that can be drawn from the criminal court data is that Carolina colonists truly engaged in a diversity of misbehavior that challenged the social order. Only a complex society, not a primitive or backward one, would generate this array of crimes. Beyond this, the data identify some fixed points in the Carolina world. There is the growing secularity of values as lawmen turned their attention from morals offenses to other crimes. The gradual decline in theft prosecutions and in charges of trespass and homicide also points to a colony emerging from its frontier beginnings, a colony that could now lay claim to a legal system that both reflected and imposed stability. There is also the problem of assault, which the courts prosecuted in great numbers and which showed itself to be an eighteenth-century fact of life. And, as subtle as its presence may be, there is also the reality of slavery. In ways that the records do not document, both actual and imagined slave crime had its impact on white justice. And just as all colonies where slavery figured, North Carolina had to juggle two criminal justice systems, one designed to produce absolute submission and one, based on centuries of law and tradition, designed to protect individuals and society from errant behavior.

IV

CRIMINAL SUSPECTS

[B]ut being moved and Seduced by the Instigation of the Devil
—Crown *v.* Branch *(1721)*

O n the night of June 16, 1727, a planter from Perquimans Precinct named Elijah Stanton broke into the home of planter Thomas Weeks and stole money and "Hogs lard or Fatt two Middle peices of Bacon and eighteen Yards of Cloth."[1] Nearly all we know about Stanton and his crime appears in a single document—the indictment. And Stanton's is typical of thousands that have survived. It tells us who the defendant is, where he lives, and where he fits, in a general way, on the social scale. What the indictment does not supply are crucial bits of evidence that would assuredly offer valuable insights into early American crime. What was Stanton's motive, for example? Did he know his victim? Who reported the crime? Who arrested the defendant? At best, answers can be pieced together from many different records; at worst, answers will never be known at all.

Over the years, thousands of criminal suspects have left their imprint, sometimes barely visible and sometimes stark, on indictments, file papers, dockets, minutes, coroners' inquests, and on reports of the Committees on Public Claims. Taken together, these documents help to delineate the contours of Carolina society and to shed some light on its neglected segments. Indeed, one of the real treasures of the court records is the evidence they give us about the all-but-invisible men and women of the colonial world. Long touted as a colony of middle-class whites, North Carolina was, in fact, the sum of many parts. This conventional

1. *Crown v. Stanton*, July, 1727, NCHCR, VI, 423–24.

description, however, had its beginnings in the eighteenth century, when observers remarked, and disdainfully, on what they saw as an excess of equality. Quoted many times in colonial histories, George Burrington complained in 1732 of a similarity "in Dress and Carriage, between the Justices, Constables and Planters that came to a Court," and of such a lack of distinction "between the Officers and Private men, at a Muster" as could be found "in no other Country but this." And as late as 1775, Scottish visitor Janet Schaw commented on what she found to be a "most disgusting equality."[2] Even most current studies of early North Carolina tend to hide the lower half by focusing on the colony's large white middle class. Women and blacks, while certainly not absent from the early literature, have only recently begun to generate historical research.[3] Here is where the criminal court records and all related data provide a fuller picture of the Carolina world, warts and all. Here the once-invisible people of that world—women, laborers, slaves—almost visibly come to life. Susana McGowan, for example, a thirty-two-year-old servant, would be lost in history had she not committed a crime. Court records of 1725 describe her as having "Black haire black complection . . . Severll Marks in her Arms . . . and a Swarthy Complection her Apparoll is a red Gown and a Spreckled Lyning Gown." Together with her servant husband, Bartholomew, an Irishman with "Much pock gotten in One of his hands," McGowan stole a long list of items including ribbons, lace, and "Bulletts." While the records say little more about the McGowans, alias the McGreens, this servant couple nevertheless leaves an imprint for posterity. Another group of people, the slaves, could not speak in a conventional way about themselves. For them, the legal records speak loudly and clearly. Records of the Committees of Public Claims, which compensated masters for executed slave criminals, name "Cesar, who was put to death for the Murder of his Master" and Dublin, hanged for killing Mr. Thomas Corprew. Evidence from the records of a freeholders court identifies "a Negro Man named

2. Burrington to Board of Trade, February 20, 1732, in *NCSR*, III, 333; Schaw, *Journal of a Lady of Quality*, 153.

3. A relatively recent article devoted to the topic of women but offering little analysis is Alan D. Watson, "Women in Colonial North Carolina," *NCHR*, LVIII (1981), 1–22. On early North Carolina as a middle-class world, see Lefler and Powell, *Colonial North Carolina*, 176; Ekirch, "Poor Carolina," 24–25; and Jackson Turner Main, *The Social Structure of Revolutionary America* (Princeton, 1965), 66. On the lack of slavery scholarship, see Crow, *The Black Experience in Revolutionary North Carolina*, vii.

Quamino . . . charged with robbing sundry Persons," who was convicted and quickly hanged.[4] When the underside of society can be identified in this way, it is possible to compare the experiences of rich and poor, black and white, male and female in the suspect population and to determine if and how these experiences changed over time.

In the course of roughly one hundred years, the Carolina courts (excluding those that tried slaves) generated data on 4,508 criminal suspects. Among these were men, women, slaves, free blacks, Indians, planters, laborers, etc. Gender identification of the accused pointed to 4,117 men (3,450 individuals), 370 women (323 individuals), and 21 people whose sex could not be determined. That male suspects greatly outnumbered female is no surprise, since to this day women continue to engage in less crime than men do. North Carolina's small percentage of accused women (8.2) nearly parallels New York's, though it is substantially smaller than what studies of other colonies have found.[5] A glance at a few criminal action papers shows that gender and status were important and deliberately noted distinctions. Men were usually identified by occupation, women by marital status. And the purposeful use of these distinctions highlights their significance. A defendant's social position, announced to judges and jury as the clerk read the indictment, was clearly meant to aid in their deliberations. A woman's marital situation, also made a matter of public information, could enable her to avoid

4. Hue and cry for McGowans, January, 1725, General Court Criminal Papers, 1720–29; *Allen* v. *Davis* and *Metcalf* v. *McGreen*, March, 1725, *NCHCR*, VI, 88; *Crown* v. *McGowans*, March, 1725, *NCHCR*, VI, 110; Report of the Committee of Public Claims, November 13, 1762, *NCSR*, VI, 741; Freeholders court, February 7, 1768, *NCSR*, VII, 685–86.

5. Rita J. Simon and Navin Sharma, "The Female Defendant in Washington, D.C., 1974–1975" (Institute for Law and Social Research, 1978), Sec. I, p. 7; Greenberg, *Crime and Law Enforcement in New York*, 51; Lyle Koehler, *A Search for Power: The "Weaker Sex" in Seventeenth-Century New England* (Urbana, 1980), 210. Of those suspected of serious crimes, 2,394 were men and 179 were women. Accused females composed, overall, 6.95 percent of the defendant population, a figure much smaller than that given in N. E. H. Hull, "Female Felons: Women and Serious Crime in the Superior Court of Massachusetts, 1673–1774" (Ph.D. dissertation, Columbia University, 1981), 136. In Richmond County, Virginia, 17.9 percent of those accused of felonious property crimes were women. See Hoffer and Scott (eds.), *Criminal Proceedings in Colonial Virginia*, lxiv. According to G. S. Rowe, "Women's Crime and Criminal Administration in Pennsylvania, 1763–1790," *Pennsylvania Magazine of History and Biography*, CIX (1985), 339, women generated 14.8 percent of all criminal charges in late eighteenth-century Pennsylvania.

TABLE 5

SOCIOECONOMIC CLASSIFICATION OF THE ACCUSED, 1663–1776

Classification	Number	Percentage
Planter	467	43.36%
Laborer	191	17.73
Gentleman	89	8.26
Artisan	63	5.85
Wife	49	4.55
Mariner	34	3.15
Merchant	23	2.13
Other[1]	161	14.94
Total	1,077	99.97

NOTE: This table is based on 1,077 accused persons whose classification is noted in the records.

[1] Thirty-one other categories include spinster, servant, single woman, captain, and lawyer.

prosecution for offenses she committed under coercion by her husband.[6]

Aside from the seven major occupational or marital classifications that appear in the records, thirty-one others reflect a broad range of socioeconomic positions (Table 5). Suspects were commonly identified as barber, carpenter, bricklayer, oysterman, plasterer, blacksmith, shoemaker, cooper, tailor, and turner. This list suggests a variety of skilled workers in the colony. Other occupations included lawyer, justice of the peace, doctor, surgeon, cleric, and schoolmaster. One category that appears frustratingly few times is *servant,* for unfree white men and women must have been far more numerous in the defendant population than the criminal court data imply. Servant suspects could be hidden by the identity of "laborer" or by their craft. And the most common servant criminal, a runaway, is not likely to appear in any formal evidence at all, since magistrates courts, which handled runaways, produced no permanent records. A few references to servant runaways appear in civil suits in which masters are seeking extra service from captured runaways to compensate for lost labor. In fact, the most profitable source of informa-

6. See Davis, *Justice of Peace,* 180.

tion about fugitive servants may be the colonial press. The *North Carolina Gazette,* for example, ran this advertisement: "Benjamin Bond, a Miller, aged about 40, of a middle Stature, much pitted with the Small-Pox, of a ruddy Complexion. Paul Price, a Baker, aged about 19 or 20, a small-fac'd well looking Lad, they are in Sailors Habits and pass as such: They have been ran away some Time from Virginia." But nothing else about these two men is known.[7]

Indians scarcely appear in the criminal court records, a result of their small number in the colony's population and the special legal proceedings established for Indians suspected of crimes. In cases of animal stealing, an Indian commissioner appointed by the governor or a magistrate, "together with the ruler or head man of the Town" to which the suspect belonged, served as the court. Indians accused of more serious crimes were tried under a special commission of oyer and terminer—a practice similar to the method of prosecuting slaves in Virginia. One of the few such courts that ever sat tried "John Cope a Christian Indian" for "Burglariously breaking and entering into the Mansion house" of Thomas Pollock in 1722. Four years later, an oyer and terminer court convicted George Senneka, a "Manherrin Indian," for the murder of Catherine Groom and her "two infant Children."[8] Given the infrequency of such cases, it would be easy to conclude that Indian inhabitants of the colony did not break the law. Or if they did, white colonists, particularly in the backcountry, where the bulk of the Indian population lived, may have dispensed their own form of justice. The rare use of special commissions could also reflect the reluctance of white authorities to impose English law on Indians. Only for the most serious Indian crimes, those that could not be ignored, did the governor convene a special court.

Free blacks appear a bit more frequently in the records than do Indians. Throughout the colonial period, their number composed from 3 to 4 percent of the total black population. More than half of these were mulattoes. The case of Mary Lewes, a "mullatto servant" accused of assaulting Debra Latham, or of John Moore, a "free Negro" also

7. See *NCSR,* XXIII, 63, 199, for servant runaways in magistrates courts. For examples of civil suits, see *Kembull v. Stradford,* July, 1708, *NCHCR,* IV, 407; and *Maule v. Sheamer,* March, 1723, *NCHCR,* V, 387. *North Carolina Gazette,* June 16, 1753.

8. *NCSR,* XXIII, 88; Rankin, *Criminal Trial Proceedings in Virginia,* 120; *Crown v. Cope,* October, 1722, *NCHCR,* V, 320–21; *Crown v. Senneka,* July, 1726, *NCHCR,* VI, 281–82. Also see *Crown v. Strawberry,* October, 1757, General Court Criminal Papers—General, Assize, and Supreme Courts, 1750–59.

charged with assault, or of Kate, a "free Negro whipped at carts-tail" for "poison," gives us no more than a snapshot of nearly the only free blacks identified as criminal suspects.[9] Their few appearances in these records simply say that at the very least they avoided one of the worst tools of black oppression, the freeholders courts, by having access to the regular courts.

Much of what is currently known about the slave criminal population is based on the work of Michael Kay and Lorin Lee Cary. Looking at claims court records, they found that between 1748 and 1772 there were 115 slaves who were executed or castrated.[10] Most slaves within this group were male field hands from large plantations (105). Slaves who ran away (records of 134 survive for the years 1748 to 1775) were also typically young, male field hands (89 percent), and a large number were African-born. In general, slave runaways had been sold to a new master and were trying to return to their previous situation. Or they might be recently imported Africans, pressed by the shock of arrival to flee. Given the potential outcome of slave crime, whether chains, castration, or death, the forces that led slaves to challenge their conditions must have been powerful indeed. A glance at a few freeholders court records leaves little doubt that for some bondspeople, crime was an act of rebellion despite its potentially death-dealing consequences. For some, crime was an act of suicide. Consider the case of Rose, a slave convicted of arson and attempted murder. In the lengthy testimony from her trial by a Halifax County slave court, a white witness said "that soon after the . . . Barn was Burn'd the Prisoner was bro.ᵗ before him on Suspicion of committing sd. fact, to be examined thereof, of that without any threats or coertion, She there Voluntarily confess'd to him that She did put fire in the Said Barn amongst some Corn Shucks." As the story unfolded, five other men testified to her guilt, including two slaves. According to "Luke a Negro Boy," Rose had "told him that if her Master whip'd her or burn'd her cloaths as he said he would, she would burn his

9. Kay and Cary, "A Demographic Analysis of Colonial North Carolina," in Crow and Hatley (eds.), *Black Americans,* 103, 110; *Crown* v. *Duncan and Lewes,* August, 1740, General Court Criminal Papers, 1740–44; *Crown* v. *Moore,* January, 1762, Craven County Court Minutes, April, 1761–July, 1762; *Crown* v. *Kate,* May, 1763, New Bern District Court Trial, Argument, Reference, and Appearance Docket, 1758–60. Also see *Crown* v. *Negroes,* July, 1769, and *Crown* v. *Massey,* November, 1770, Johnston County Court Minutes, 1767–77.

10. Kay and Cary, " 'They are Indeed the Constant Plague,' " 37–56. Also see Kay and Cary, "Slave Runaways in Colonial North Carolina," 1–39; and Crow, *The Black Experience in Revolutionary North Carolina,* Chap. 3.

House over his Head & then kill herself." In 1740 a slave named Harry, charged with raping a sixteen-year-old girl, "being asked whither he Lay with the sd Mary Declared he Did." This simple statement speaks vividly to the hopeless situation of accused slaves. Finally, there is the haunting case of "a certain Negro Will." According to a deposition of Thomas Hall given in 1769, Will "had declared that he would Poison Mrs. Lucy Hall," his wife. Once in custody, Will admitted that "he did intend to have given a Dose of something to the said Mrs. Hall," and two hours later "did himself take the same Dose of Poison which he had intended to administer to Mrs. Hall & that he died thereof." In light of such cases, it is difficult to avoid concluding that slave criminals showed a combination of rebelliousness and self-destruction, two characteristics that drew on their own inner strength and on the innate frailty of the slave system itself.[11]

The bulk of the evidence on North Carolina crime derives from the activities of white men. Among them, *planter* was the most common status. All planters owned land, but their holdings were of no particular size. They could be wealthy or men of lesser means, but had one thing in common—ownership of real property. Gentlemen, artisans, and merchants also appear in the records quite often. Not necessarily men of wealth, they still enjoyed a standard of living above that of lower-class colonists. Two socioeconomic labels, laborer and mariner, which also account for a substantial portion of all status identities, describe men at or near the bottom of the social strata.[12]

When prosecution rates for planters and laborers are compared, a striking if not predictable pattern emerges (Table 6). Overall, the courts prosecuted more poor men for theft and animal stealing. Conversely, the most common accusations against men of means were assault, crimes against morality, and contempt. We would expect the poor to engage in a large proportion of property crime, but interestingly enough, this was not always true. Beginning in the 1750s, the courts charged many more planters with theft. The rate, much higher than that for laborers, fell off slightly in the next decade (Table 7). Here is a convincing bit of evidence

11. *Crown v. Rose*, n.d., Halifax District Court Miscellaneous Records, 1763–1808; *Crown v. Harry*, July, 1740, and Deposition of T. Hall, August, 1769, both in Secretary of State, Court Records, Magistrates and Freeholders Courts.

12. Jacob, *Law Dictionary*; Main, *The Social Structure of Revolutionary America*, 72–75, 88; Whittenburg, "Planters, Merchants, and Lawyers," 228–29; Aubrey C. Land, "Economic Base and Social Structure: The Northern Chesapeake in the Eighteenth Century," *Journal of Economic History*, XXV (1965), 639–54.

TABLE 6

PROSECUTIONS, BY SOCIOECONOMIC STATUS, 1663–1776

| | | | | | | Percentage Prosecuted | | | | |
Classification	Number	Assault	Theft	Morals Crimes	Trespass	Animal Stealing	Contempt	Crimes Against Order	Homicide	Other
Planter	467	35.12%	17.56%	4.28%	4.50%	10.06%	7.49%	2.35%	4.71%	13.93%
Laborer	191	26.70	25.13	2.61	2.62	15.18	2.09	3.66	4.19	17.82
Gentleman	89	38.20	15.73	4.49	—	—	4.49	3.37	2.25	31.47
Artisan	63	34.92	15.87	11.11	—	1.59	11.11	3.17	7.94	14.29
Wife	49	38.78	24.49	8.16	4.08	2.04	2.04	—	—	20.40
Mariner	34	26.47	44.12	—	—	—	5.88	—	5.88	17.65
Merchant	23	26.09	17.39	4.34	4.35	—	13.04	4.34	—	30.45
Other[1]	161	18.63	18.01	13.66	3.10	1.24	4.34	1.24	9.31	30.43

NOTE: "Other" column includes twenty-nine other different charges.

[1] Includes thirty-one other socioeconomic categories.

TABLE 7
PROSECUTIONS, BY DECADE, FOR PLANTERS AND LABORERS

Crime	1720s		1730s		1740s		1750s		1760s	
	P	L	P	L	P	L	P	L	P	L
Assault	1 (6.25%)	1 (10.00%)	48 (42.86%)	9 (25.00%)	55 (47.83%)	8 (42.11%)	11 (45.83%)	5 (55.56%)	26 (39.39%)	16 (31.37%)
Theft	2 (12.50)	6 (60.00)	25 (22.32)	18 (50.00)	23 (20.00)	9 (47.37)	8 (33.33)	1 (11.11)	15 (22.73)	11 (21.57)
Animal Stealing	—	—	7 (6.25)	5 (13.89)	15 (13.04)	1 (5.26)	1 (4.17)	1 (11.11)	14 (21.21)	20 (39.22)
Contempt	11 (68.75)	1 (10.00)	15 (13.39)	2 (5.56)	1 (0.87)	—	2 (8.32)	—	4 (6.06)	1 (1.96)
Other[1]	2 (12.50)	2 (20.00)	17 (15.18)	2 (5.56)	21 (18.27)	1 (5.26)	2 (8.32)	2 (22.22)	7 (10.61)	3 (5.88)

[1]Includes homicide, adultery/fornication, bastardy, and trespassing.

of the colony's growing economic complexity. Men of means could now find items they regarded as worth stealing.

Gentlemen, planters, and artisans were charged with assault in much higher proportions than were poor men. Such was true in Elizabethan Essex, where men of means committed the largest proportion of violent crimes.[13] At first glance, these findings contradict the perception that the poor lead more violent lives. But perhaps the violent behavior of upper-crust colonists was scrutinized more carefully by their peers on the court. A better understanding of the link between violence and status may emerge from a decade-by-decade analysis of assault prosecutions. Laborers were not, in fact, always charged with assault at lower rates than were planters. In the 1720s and 1750s, for example, they were actually accused of assault in larger proportions. But in the 1760s the courts once again charged planters with assault at a higher rate than that for laborers. Since there is no obvious pattern of change, assault prosecution rates for planters and laborers were not significantly different. In the white male population, personal violence occurred no more or less often among men of means than among those who had little or nothing.

A better-defined relationship is evident between status and moral misbehavior. Not only were planters charged with crimes against morality at an average of twice the rate for laborers, but they were also charged with different kinds of morals crimes. Admittedly, none of these offenses represented a major portion of accusations for either group, since summary courts could handle some of these breaches out of term. In nearly one hundred years, charges of adultery, fornication, and bastardy brought into court only one laborer and fourteen planters. Could the unlikely case be true that poor men led more virtuous lives? More to the point, the poor, transients with empty purses, left lawmen indifferent to their moral misbehavior. Men of property, who had resources and some permanence in their community, risked the exposure of their personal conduct to the legal system and to a certain amount of probing by neighbors.

The clearest link between status and crime exists in cases of contempt. In fact, between 1720 and 1776, there is evidence in the records of only four contempt charges against laborers and two against mariners. And for every decade beginning in 1720, contempt charges brought planters into court at a much higher rate than laborers. This

13. Joel Samaha, *Law and Order in Historical Perspective: The Case of Elizabethan Essex* (New York, 1974), 27–28.

pattern was true for other antigovernment offenses—sedition and perjury. Nearly the only men accused of these crimes were planters, gentlemen, surgeons, and doctors. Despite the current perception of weak deferential attitudes in early Carolina, the data here show that poor men deferred to authority as much as those of greater means resisted it. Among the poor, deference was in fact strong. Especially in the 1720s and 1730s, at the height of political strife, North Carolina's emerging elite showed little of that submission to authority.[14]

Recidivists certainly appeared among planters and laborers, but the rate at which men from these two groups returned to court scarcely differed. Among 338 individual planters accused of crimes, 93 were charged more than once. In a group of 130 individual laborer defendants, 35 were recidivists. Most men in both groups returned to court two or three times. Law enforcement proved to be as ineffective in deterring crime among planters as among men of lesser means.

The records contain evidence of relationships between status and crime, and between gender and crime as well. Even though the courts largely prosecuted men, comparisons of male and female crime help clarify what is currently known about colonial North Carolina women. Early accounts of the female population are sparse. Virtually no demographic data exist to help determine the sex composition of the colony at any particular time. A study of early Perquimans County describes an equal proportion of men and women there, but evidence is too scarce to suggest generalizations about the colony as a whole. One rare contemporary clue appears in John Lawson's 1709 assertion that women of the colony married very young and "She that stays single till Twenty, is reckon'd a stale Maid; which is a very indifferent Character in that warm Country." Since teenage marriages for women generally reflect a high sex ratio, the earliest North Carolina population may have been largely male. As the colony grew, it would be safe to assume that the proportion of women in the population increased. An incomplete census for 1786, the first that specifies females, shows a nearly equal number of white men and women in the state.[15]

14. On deference, see Ekirch, "*Poor Carolina*," 32; and Eli Faber, "Puritan Criminals: The Economic, Social, and Intellectual Background to Crime in Seventeenth-Century Massachusetts," *Perspectives in American History*, XI (1977–78), 120.

15. James M. Gallman, "Determinants of Age at Marriage in Colonial Perquimans County, North Carolina," *WMQ*, 3rd ser., XXXIX (1982), 178; John Lawson, *A New Voyage to Carolina*, ed. Hugh T. Lefler (Chapel Hill, 1967), 91; Daniel Scott Smith, "The Demographic History of Colonial New England," *Journal of Economic History*, XXXII (1972), 176; Greene and Harrington, *American Population*, 169.

A little can be learned about Carolina women from the few contemporary observations that survive. In 1711, missionary John Urmston described the women of the colony as hard workers who engaged in "all trades . . . within their spheres, becoming Soap makers Starch makers Dyes &c." John Lawson was impressed by their "good Houswifry," their excellent health, and remarkable fertility. At the end of the colonial period, Scotswoman Janet Schaw found the upper-class women of Wilmington to be "Amiable" and "agreeable . . . many of whom would make a figure in any part of the world." And just a few years later, the well-known traveler Francisco de Miranda lamented, "The married women of New Bern maintain a monastic seclusion and submission to their husbands as I have never seen." But Miranda also noted that the single women "enjoy complete freedom."[16] These comments, however, reveal nothing distinctive about Carolina women. Like their counterparts elsewhere in America, they submitted to their husbands and worked "within their spheres." Those few who did not, those who severed their female bonds by committing crimes, offer a fruitful means of learning more about the rest.

North Carolina data on female crime seem to support the long-held belief that women engage in less crime than men do.[17] Not only did they represent a small proportion of the defendant population, but they also returned to the courts at nearly half the male rate.[18] Yet the small proportion of female crime and the low rate of recidivism need not mean that women committed fewer crimes. A high sex ratio could easily explain the low female crime rate. So could a certain amount of paternalism, which might allow some women to evade prosecution; others could be shielded by the law of coverture. At common law a woman found stealing with her husband could not be indicted "because of the Necessity of Obedience" unless "it was at his Persuasion, without Constraint." It is impossible to know how many women coverture actually protected from prosecution. Some courts apparently evaded the law by

16. John Urmston to [?], July, 1711, in *NCSR*, I, 764; Lawson, *A New Voyage*, 91; Schaw, *Journal of a Lady of Quality*, 154; Francisco de Miranda, *The New Democracy in America*, trans. Judson P. Wood, ed. John S. Ezell (Norman, 1963), 5–6.

17. See J. M. Beattie, "The Criminality of Women in Eighteenth-Century England," *Journal of Social History*, VIII (1975), 82; and Rowe, "Women's Crime and Criminal Administration in Pennsylvania," 364.

18. For the entire colonial period, 666 individuals were charged more than once. Of these, 629 were men and 37 were women. The rate of recidivism for men was 18.23 percent (629÷3,450); for women, 11.45 percent (37÷323). In a study of Massachusetts females accused of serious crimes, Hull found a recidivism rate of 8.5 percent, though she suspects that the rate was actually higher. See Hull, "Female Felons," 104.

identifying married female suspects as "spinster." In 1725, for example, the General Court indicted an accused thief, Susana McGowan, "Wife of the Sayd Bartholomew spinster."[19] Sparse as the evidence is, it appears that Carolina courts ignored the constraints of coverture by assuming that wives joined husbands in crime without coercion. Coverture notwithstanding, spouses were together charged with crimes in thirty-two cases.

Unlike men, for whom assault was the most common crime, the largest proportion of female suspects were charged with moral misbehavior (Table 8). This characteristic of female crime persisted throughout the colonial period (Table 9). Lest Carolina women appear to show a uniquely low level of morality, or the courts a bias toward prosecuting female immorality, suffice it to say that this pattern of female morals prosecutions was common in other colonies. In seventeenth-century New England, which admittedly practiced enforcement of morals intensely, nearly 42 percent of female criminal suspects were accused of morals crimes. A New York study found that a much higher proportion of women than men came to court for moral misbehavior. Comparing North Carolina higher court data with parallel data for colonial Massachusetts indicates that the northern courts prosecuted 0.9 percent of all male and 13.4 percent of all female suspects for crimes against morality. In North Carolina, 2.4 percent of all male suspects were charged with adultery or fornication, as were 16.2 percent of all accused females.[20]

Given the status of colonial women and the kinds of lives they led, it would be surprising if moral misbehavior were not a common female criminal charge. Unable to engage in other kinds of crime, women could break the moral code without stepping out of their prescribed boundaries. This is the conventional explanation for the typically large proportion of female morals crimes. Yet other possibilities are worth considering. Women, for example, engaged in fewer kinds of crimes than did men (twenty-six for women and forty-three for men). Social norms,

19. Beattie, "The Criminality of Women," 95–96; Davis, *Justice of Peace*, 180; Carol Z. Wiener, "Is a Spinster an Unmarried Woman?" *AJLH*, XX (1976), 27–31; *Crown* v. *McGowans*, March, 1725, NCHCR, VI, 110.

20. Koehler, *A Search for Power*, 193; Greenberg, *Crime and Law Enforcement in New York*, 51; Hull, "Female Felons," 114. The North Carolina data identify 29 women charged with adultery or fornication in a suspect population of 179, and 58 males in a suspect population of 2,394. I considered only higher court records, in order to make a more accurate comparison with Hull's data.

TABLE 8
PROSECUTIONS, BY SEX, 1663–1776

| | | | | | | | Percentage Prosecuted | | | |
Sex	Number	Assault	Theft	Morals Crimes	Trespass	Animal Stealing	Contempt	Crimes Against Public Order	Homicide	Other
Male	4,117	31.67%	12.58%	7.01%	6.41%	5.95%	3.79%	3.64%	2.48%	26.47%
Female	370	20.54	17.03	31.62	2.97	.81	1.35	2.43	4.05	19.18
All suspects	4,487	30.76	12.95	9.04	6.13	5.53	3.59	3.54	2.61	25.75

NOTE: "Other" includes at least thirty other different charges.

TABLE 9
PROSECUTIONS, BY DECADE, FOR MEN AND WOMEN

Crime	1720s		1730s		1740s		1750s		1760s	
	M	W	M	W	M	W	M	W	M	W
Assault	9 (10.48%)	—	99 (37.64%)	14 (17.39%)	137 (41.27%)	14 (24.56%)	232 (56.86%)	13 (30.23%)	520 (53.72%)	31 (38.27%)
Theft	26 (31.71)	13 (48.15%)	72 (27.38)	12 (52.17)	65 (19.58)	4 (7.02)	56 (13.73)	6 (13.95)	167 (17.25)	20 (24.69)
Adultery/ Forn.	6 (7.32)	5 (18.52)	12 (4.56)	2 (8.70)	30 (9.04)	30 (52.63)	28 (6.86)	18 (41.86)	49 (5.06)	13 (16.05)
Bastardy	1 (1.22)	4 (14.81)	4 (1.52)	2 (8.70)	2 (0.60)	7 (12.28)	2 (0.49)	1 (2.33)	3 (0.31)	6 (7.41)
Other[1]	40 (48.78)	5 (18.52)	76 (28.90)	3 (13.05)	98 (29.52)	2 (3.51)	90 (22.06)	5 (11.63)	229 (23.66)	11 (13.57)

[1]Includes contempt, homicide, animal stealing, and trespass.

which placed women in a subordinate role, may have led to their more rigorous prosecution for moral misbehavior. Indeed, for one morals offense—bastardy—women were more likely to appear in the court records than were their male partners. While the records underestimate the total number of bastardy cases, they reveal a lopsided number of twenty-two actions against men and twenty-eight against women. Unlike women who carried the condemning evidence with them, named fathers could escape prosecution. Furthermore, as the law provided, a woman could be punished for bastardy, but not so her male partner who was to support the child.[21] Men would appear in court only if they denied paternity or failed to provide for their offspring.

The preponderance of morals charges among female crimes is especially striking when gender comparisons are made for adultery and fornication. These two offenses composed 23 percent of all charges against women and only 3 percent of all male charges. Even when changes over time are considered, the sharp difference in prosecution rates is the same (see Table 9). The evidence seems, then, to support the consensus that a double standard operated in eighteenth-century America, one that led to a greater toleration of certain sexual activities of men. But perhaps there is a different story. Between 1663 and 1776, the courts charged 165 men and 85 women with adultery and fornication. Since the records rarely name the partner of the accused, at least some men were prosecuted while their female partners apparently were not. Other fragmentary evidence suggests a double standard that in fact worked to the advantage of women. In four cases, for example, the female partner of the accused is identified but not prosecuted herself.[22] Furthermore, 6 women and 52 men faced charges while their partners did not. Since adultery, by law, had to involve a married woman, perhaps juries deferred to husbands by indicting only the adulterer. Or perhaps married women escaped prosecution because they were seen as victims of seduction rather than as offenders against morality. In light of comparable data for Massachusetts, it appears that the courts did indeed favor adulteresses. More Carolina men than women were prosecuted for adultery—an offense that by definition should have an equal number of

21. See Walter J. King, "Punishment for Bastardy in Early Seventeenth-Century England," *Albion*, X (1978), 134.
22. *Crown v. Freeman*, September, 1764, Salisbury District Court Criminal Action Papers, 1760–71; *Crown v. Parker*, March, 1766, Salisbury District Court Trial and Minute Docket, 1761–90; *Crown v. Downing*, 1731, General Court Criminal Papers, 1730–34; *Crown v. Boude*, March, 1736, General Court Criminal Papers, 1735–37.

male and female suspects. The Massachusetts courts charged more women than men.[23] Such limited evidence is far from conclusive, but it tends to stress the importance of female social constraints to the North while diminishing their importance to the South.

If women suspected of adultery could expect leniency from the courts, those accused of fornication could not. The records of the Carolina courts and of seventeenth-century Salem's courts reveal that male and female fornicators were prosecuted in nearly equal numbers.[24] This is slender but tantalizing evidence of different treatment for single and married women. A married offender against morality might evade formal punishment, but a single woman who broke the moral code would not. She was a marginal figure in her community, and when she stepped beyond proper behavior, she threatened to burden the taxpayers with an illegitimate child.

Overall, evidence gleaned from the Carolina records does not present a convincing picture of harsher treatment for the female defendant population. That women were prosecuted for adultery, fornication, and bastardy in greater proportions than were men says that women avoided other kinds of crimes that attracted men. Moreover, only a select group of morals offenses actually brought women into court. With the exceptions of one case of swearing and three of keeping a disorderly house, female crime suspects faced the kind of sex-related charges that women could commit without actually violating their private domestic role. Female prosecutions for assault illustrate this point. Although women were accused of this offense in much smaller proportions than were men, assault was still the second-most-common charge for women.[25] This fact alone seems to contradict the norm of female passiveness. Yet assaults by women did not duplicate precisely those by men. Since the county courts tried a higher proportion of female assault cases, women engaged in less serious bouts of violence than men did (Table 10). They attacked other women, men, neighbors, but assaults on figures of au-

23. In the North Carolina higher courts, 26 men were charged with adultery; 15 women were so charged. In the parallel Massachusetts courts, 8 men and 30 women were charged. See Hull, "Female Felons," 99.

24. In North Carolina, 30 men and 27 women were charged. In Salem, there were court appearances by 201 males and 206 females. See C. Dallett Hemphill, "Women in Court: Sex-Role Differentiation in Salem, Massachusetts, 1636–1683," *WMQ*, 3rd. ser., XXXIX (1982), 166.

25. High female assault rates were also true for Massachusetts and New York. See Hull, "Female Felons," 114; and Greenberg, *Crime and Law Enforcement in New York*, 50.

TABLE 10

SELECTED CHARGES, BY COURT AND SEX, 1670–1776

Court	Assault		Theft		Adultery/Fornication	
	M	F	M	F	M	F
General	253 (19.40%)	16 (21.05%)	191 (36.87%)	32 (50.79%)	43 (26.06%)	29 (34.12%)
Supreme	86 (6.60)	2 (2.63)	37 (7.14)	3 (4.76)	—	—
Superior	314 (24.08)	12 (15.79)	129 (24.90)	11 (17.46)	15 (9.09)	—
County	634 (48.62)	46 (60.53)	143 (27.61)	17 (26.98)	107 (64.85)	56 (65.88)
County Court of Albermarle	17 (1.30)	—	18 (3.48)	—	—	—

thority, such as law enforcement officials, were rare. The lower prosecution rate and the character of the victims indicate that within their sphere, women did not act as aggressively as men did. Those who acted aggressively at all were among the few who dared to challenge the sex-role expectations in their society.

One crime that women could easily commit without doing damage to female constraints was theft. It was not, however, a largely female crime—the courts prosecuted 89 percent of all thefts against men. Yet a larger proportion of all female suspects than of male suspects was accused of theft. Like female colonists in New York and Massachusetts who were also suspected of stealing in proportionally high numbers, North Carolina thieves were servants, ordinary keepers, and single women who had access to the household items commonly named in their indictments.[26] Women rarely engaged in animal stealing, which required the freedom of movement available only to men. It would be difficult to conclude, given the incompleteness of the data, that most female theft suspects were driven by grinding poverty to steal. Yet the evidence from the records offers a slight hint of a link between poverty and one particular group of women—the unmarried. Of the nineteen female suspects identified as either a spinster or single, the courts charged at least eight with property crimes.

No other crime better illustrates the desperate plight of some women than murder, for women were often accused of killing a newborn child. Studies that look carefully into infanticide, a largely female crime, speculate about motivation and find common patterns of prosecution.[27] Murder in any form was not a familiar female crime. Only fifteen female murder suspects are identified in the records. But at least six of these cases involved an infant death. The grimmest of records describe single and married women who tried to conceal pregnancies and births, and were then indicted for strangling or drowning their offspring. In 1735 the General Court jury acquitted Ann Morris, a spinster, of suffocating her five-day-old son. Ten years later, Ann Sumner, also a spinster, was accused of choking her infant daughter to death. Mary Gorman, a

26. Greenberg, *Crime and Law Enforcement in New York*, 50; Hull, "Female Felons," 114.
27. Julia Cherry Spruill, *Women's Life and Work in the Southern Colonies* (1938; rpr. New York, 1972), 323; Rankin, *Criminal Trial Proceedings in Virginia*, 205–206; Koehler, *A Search for Power*, 199; Peter C. Hoffer and N. E. H. Hull, *Murdering Mothers: Infanticide in England and New England, 1558–1803* (New York, 1981); Rowe, "Women's Crime and Criminal Administration in Pennsylvania," 343.

spinster and a servant, escaped conviction for drowning her "Bastard child." Still another single woman, Magdalen Collar, hanged for burying alive a child she had just delivered.[28] As gruesome as these cases are, they were rare. Either infanticide was not a serious problem in the colony or women who killed their babies managed to avoid detection. Moreover, four of the recorded cases occurred in a single decade, the 1720s, and none after 1750. But instances of infant killing are nevertheless worth noting for what they have to say about the accused. Within the small available sample is a disproportionate number of single women. The intense social and economic pressures that drove them, perhaps abandoned by their mates, to murder their offspring can only be imagined.

The offenses that scarcely ever appear among female suspects bring into sharper focus the existence of separate sexual spheres. Seldom do the records contain evidence of women accused of riot, affray, or other offenses against public order. Ann Hammond, convicted of breach of peace in 1740, and Elizabeth Fugg of riot in 1768, represent two of the ten female charges for this category of crime.[29] Nor were women often charged with other kinds of "public" crimes. Contempt of authority brought a total of five females into court, and sedition brought one. Forgery and counterfeiting, two kinds of commercial crimes, resulted in only four prosecutions against women. Neither were women often accused of jail escape or nuisance. This kind of evidence serves as well as any to underscore the reality of two worlds divided by gender. Confined to a private sphere apart from men, women surely had fewer opportunities to engage in public or commercial crime. The locus of their activity was within the family and the home, far from the public arena.

Women's status in the colony may have been a step below that of men, but it was never static. Beginning in the 1740s, for example, the proportion of females accused of certain morals crimes steadily declined.[30] This change was part of the same colony-wide pattern of de-

28. R. W. Malcolmson, "Infanticide in the Eighteenth Century," in Cockburn (ed.), *Crime in England*, 193–96; *Crown v. Morris*, October, 1735, General Court Criminal Papers, 1735–37; *Crown v. Sumner*, March, 1745, General Court Criminal Papers—General and Assize Courts, 1745–49; *Crown v. Gorman*, October, 1726, NCHCR, VI, 324; *Crown v. Collar*, March, 1720, NCHCR, V, 212–13.

29. *Crown v. Hammond*, March, 1740, Craven County Court Minutes, 1730–46; *Crown v. Fugg et al.*, November, 1768, Edenton District Court Crown Docket Superior Court, May, 1765–October, 1769.

30. The figures are 57.8 percent in 1740; 34.5 percent in 1750; and 16 percent in 1760.

TABLE 11
DEFENDANT POPULATION, BY DECADE

Decade	Men		Women	
1720s	160	(84.21%)	30	(15.78%)
1730s	358	(92.03)	31	(7.96)
1740s	482	(88.27)	64	(11.72)
1750s	613	(91.76)	55	(8.23)
1760s	1,476	(92.53)	119	(7.46)

cline in morals prosecutions. It may also be true that as the number of women more closely approached the number of men, domestic life became more stable. At the same time, as puzzling as this may seem, the prosecution rate for female assault suspects suggests a changing role for women in the colony at large. Court records of the 1720s contain not a single case of female assault. By the 1760s, the records show, 38 percent of all charges against women involved personal violence. Without reading too much into the records, we find it difficult not to conclude that women were becoming more aggressive. Perhaps their ever-developing society gave them more opportunities to assert themselves or generated new frustrations that they alleviated in a physical way. Unfortunately, the data equivocate a bit on precisely how female status was changing in the eighteenth century. What does it mean when the proportion of assault charges against women increased while the ratio of theft charges declined? There may in fact be a connection. Perhaps less female theft, overall, reflected a contraction of the female sphere, which in turn led to more aggressive female behavior. If the records do outline firmly one aspect of female prosecutions, it is that as the proportion of women in the general population increased, their proportion in the suspect population declined (Table 11). This small bit of evidence suggests that North Carolina was emerging in the modern world. There is some risk in applying inferences from criminal records to the population at large, but Carolina women were apparently duplicating the way of life of women elsewhere in America. Fewer were violating the moral boundaries of their sphere, and fewer still were challenging social constraints.

V

DISPOSITION OF CASES

She putt her Self upon the Country
    —Crown *v.* Branch *(1721)*

Perhaps the most revealing and at the same time most baffling element of law enforcement is the outcome of cases. Race, crime, gender, and status all influenced the findings of the courts. What we cannot know precisely is the extent to which these variables actually swayed decision making. Most of the available legal records offer no explicit help. They are completely silent on private jury deliberations, largely silent on trial testimony, and have little to say about judicial thinking. But jury verdicts, recorded thousands of times on presentments, indictments, and dockets, at least give us a landmark. They clarify and reflect, more than is possible with other kinds of analytical tools, the links between crime and race, gender, and status. These links open one more window on the Carolina world.

Over the years, the Carolina courts reached many different judgments, the five most common of which are listed in Table 12. A ruling of *Ignoramus* meant that the grand jury did not find a true bill, and litigation usually went no further. Dismissals resulted when defendants, witnesses, prosecutors, or jurors failed to appear, or when evidence was lacking. Judges also dismissed charges on technical points. John Hassell, an inveterate troublemaker, was accused of uttering "Blasphemous words and Discorses," but the court discharged him, without further explanation, "for Insufficiency in the Indictment."[1] The judgment "Unknown" is an artificial one, devised to encompass all those criminal charges that disappeared from the records because a judgment

---

1. *Crown* v. *Hassell*, July, 1719, *NCHCR*, V, 202, 215.

TABLE 12

DISPOSITION OF CHARGES, 1670–1776

Charge	Number	Ignoramus	Convicted	Acquitted	Dismissed	Unknown
Assault	1,378	23.43%	31.93%	8.85%	4.93%	30.84%
Theft	582	22.16	23.02	17.86	8.41	28.52
Contempt	160	13.75	25.62	4.37	9.37	46.87
Homicide	118	21.18	33.05	22.88	1.69	21.18
Morals crimes	403	2.97	22.33	7.94	20.09	46.65
Crimes against order	162	5.55	14.19	8.02	39.50	32.71
Trespass	275	25.45	20.72	16.72	5.09	32.00
Animal stealing	249	22.08	19.27	21.68	10.04	26.90
Total	3,327	19.38	26.20	12.17	9.55	32.67
All charges	4,491	18.61	25.91	13.62	9.55	32.28

NOTE: This analysis includes all cases brought before the grand jury, whether true bills were found or not. Charges that failed to go to trial can thereby be considered.

was never reached, never recorded, the parties settled their differences out of court, or the records were lost.[2]

The disposition of the eight most commonly prosecuted criminal offenses is considered here because they offer the best insights into how colonial institutions handled crime. Perhaps most striking overall is the large proportion of no bills for all but two offenses (Table 13). Grand juries clearly played a powerful role, beyond their power to present, in criminal proceedings. While their task was "to be thoroughly persuaded of the truth of an indictment, so far as their evidence goes," the records give the distinct impression that these groups responded in a variety of ways to different charges.[3] They discharged nearly one-third of the suspects whose cases came before them. Four offenses in particular— trespass, assault, theft, and animal stealing—weighed heavily among

2. In addition to the categories listed in Table 12, a few judgments appear in the records only rarely. For example, Richard Miller, servant, had his murder conviction reversed when his master, Thomas Stanton, was tried for the crime. See *Crown v. Miller*, August, 1700, *NCHCR*, III, 371–72, 377, 387–88; and *Crown v. Stanton*, August, 1700, *NCHCR*, III, 373–74, 389–90. On another occasion, the same General Court "reversed" the conviction of James Welch for killing a steer. Welch argued that the steer had been placed in his care. See *Crown v. Welch et al.*, August, 1700, *NCHCR*, III, 372. Mistrials also occurred, though only one example appears in all the court records. See *Crown v. McCarky*, September, 1752, General Court Minutes, 1750–67.

3. Blackstone, *Commentaries*, IV, 300.

TABLE 13

DISPOSITION OF CHARGES WITH KNOWN OUTCOMES, 1670–1776

Charge	Number	Ignoramus	Convicted	Acquitted	Dismissed
Assault	953	33.89%	46.16%	12.80%	7.13%
Theft	416	31.00	32.21	25.00	11.77
Contempt	85	25.88	48.23	8.23	17.64
Homicide	93	26.88	41.93	29.03	2.15
Morals crimes	215	5.58	41.86	14.88	37.67
Crimes against order	109	8.25	21.10	11.92	58.71
Trespass	187	37.43	30.48	24.59	7.48
Animal stealing	182	30.21	26.37	29.67	13.73
Total	2,240	28.79	38.92	18.08	14.19
All charges	3,041	27.49	38.27	20.12	14.10

the no bills. Since trespass comprised any number of usually minor offenses, it would be difficult to find a precise explanation for a high rate of *Ignoramus* judgments. Not so for cases of assault. Given the personal basis for many assaults, it may be that victims and attackers worked out their differences before grand jurors had a chance to hear them or that many assault charges were frivolous ones generated by anger or revenge. There are two reasons why colonists suspected of theft and animal stealing could expect a favorable outcome from the grand jury. First, these were typically difficult crimes to prove. Second, while it is virtually impossible to document, harsh penalties for theft must have swayed the jurors. On the other side of the coin, offenses against morality and public order produced a large proportion of true bills. In view of the evidence we have, it would be tempting to say that grand jurors found these behaviors repugnant and wanted the suspects to go to trial. Yet a more likely explanation has to do with the crimes themselves. Grand jurors had solid evidence to consider for these offenses—an unmarried couple living together, an illegitimate birth, a riot, or an affray. These were physical acts for which conviction did not depend, as in the case of property crime, on the identification or recovery of stolen goods.

Petit jury decisions also fall into certain discernible patterns. Four offenses—contempt, assault, homicide, and moral misconduct—all resulted in high conviction rates. This can mean nothing more than that grand juries did an effective job of screening out weak charges. At the same time, more subtle inferences can be made from the data. Assault was the offense combining all the elements that might lead to conviction. Grand juries had already dismissed the frivolous cases. Typically small fines did not discourage jurors from finding guilt. And most important, roughly 25 percent of all assault defendants pleaded guilty.[4] Did much behind-the-scenes discussion lead to these confessions? While there is no explicit evidence, a form of plea-bargaining certainly went on. This practice was known in seventeenth-century England, and was even encouraged in eighteenth-century North Carolina. In his practitioner's manual, James Davis spoke to the many "trifling Assaults" that demand the courts' attention and advised a defendant "not to put himself to the Expence of trying the Indictment," but rather to plead guilty and pay the penalty. In cases where the defendant and the accuser talked before trial and worked out "a Satisfaction," the court set a small fine.[5]

The large proportion of convictions for morals offenders can be tied to the usually minor penalties for these misdemeanors and their relatively high visibility. Moreover, the potentially burdensome impact of moral misconduct on a community—an illegitimate child—surely deterred jurors from sparing the accused. When juries returned a high proportion of guilty verdicts for men accused of contempt, they were expressing some fundamental attitudes of their world. Most contempt cases came in the early eighteenth century, a time of real internal strife. High conviction rates for contempt reflected the urgent need to control antigovernment behavior, whether politically motivated or not. Perhaps more than any other crime, contempt posed a bold challenge to government and society. No court could afford to be any less then exacting in handling this offense. Nor did courts give any indication of leniency in homicide cases. Rates of conviction were high because murder demanded immediate retribution not just for the victim but for the society at large. In addition, coroner's juries helped collect and assess evidence, assistance not available in other criminal investigations.

If petit juries effectively disposed of morals crimes, assault, contempt, and homicide, their record on property crimes was not nearly as

4. Of 1,299 charges for assault, 321 guilty pleas were recorded. The number of recorded confessions for all other crimes is so small as to have no significant effect on the conviction rate. There were only five offenses—assault, crimes against morality, trespass, contempt, and nuisance—for which defendants pleaded guilty more than ten times. Of these five, assault was the only crime for which more than forty confessions were recorded.

5. Baker, "Criminal Courts and Procedure at Common Law," in Cockburn (ed.), *Crime in England*, 35; Davis, *Justice of Peace*, 323–24.

good. For practical reasons, these were difficult crimes to prove. Witnesses were scarce, and law enforcers had no easy task of linking the accused with stolen items, particularly in a colony of substantial size and relatively sparse population. Moreover, harsh penalties, sometimes even death, doubtless pushed some jurors to the side of leniency. There is no mystery about the low conviction rate for crimes against public order. A large proportion arose from the Sugar Creek riots of 1765, and the Salisbury District Court dismissed the charges.[6]

Perhaps the most telling category of case dispositions is "Dismissed," which comprised a variety of judgments that say something about the pitfalls of colonial law enforcement. Clerks normally did not elaborate on the reasons for dismissals, but the records do leave the impression that one problem in particular left many cases unresolved—negligent jurymen. Required by law to attend a designated court session, jurors began avoiding their duty as early as 1685. In that year, John Wilson, juryman, was fined 5s. for "absenting himself without the Leave of the Court." Wilson was one of the first of a long line of jurors who, for one reason or another, failed to show up. By 1706, the persistence of incomplete juries led to a 10s. fine, raised again to 30s. in 1723, and to £5 in 1727. Later legislation on jury fines showed that the problem went on and on.[7] In the 1750s, political strife only exacerbated it. An apparently distraught Bishop Spangenburg noted that in the "older counties" the "citizens do not appear as jurors, and if court is held to decide . . . criminal matters no one is present." Negligent jurors hampered the criminal process, and so did absent witnesses. Once again, the records point to this problem in only a small way (fewer than thirty times), but legislation providing for substantial fines suggests its magnitude. During a single session of the General Court in 1725, Thomas Cook, bricklayer, was dismissed from his charge of contempt because no one appeared "to prosecute or give Evidence against him," and accused counterfeiter James Speir was discharged "for want of Evidence."[8] Five other cases also abruptly ended because "no person" appeared.

Still another thorn in the side of law enforcement was the disap-

6. See Salisbury District Court Trial and Minute Docket, 1761–90.

7. Court session, November, 1685, *NCHCR,* II, 364; 1706 fine, *NCHCR,* IV, 309; 1723 fine, *NCSR,* XXV, 184–90; 1727 fine, Colonial Office Ser. 5, Vol. 293, Public Record Office, London; later legislation, *NCSR,* XXIII, 289–91, XXV, 296.

8. Diary of Bishop Spangenburg, September 12, 1752, in *NCSR,* IV, 1311–12; 1715 and 1746 fines, *NCSR,* XXIII, 20, 261; General Court, July, 1725, *NCHCR,* VI, 143–44.

pearance of defendants. In July, 1727, the General Court cited eleven defendants who failed to show up for trial. In each case the court issued a *Capias,* but subsequent records indicate that nearly all were eventually removed from the docket. William Davis' experience, then, was not uncommon. The General Court in 1744 brought no resolution to his felony charge because Davis, a laborer, was "not to be found."[9] Perhaps most frustrating to law enforcers were those cases, explicitly cited by clerks, that were "put off the docket."[10] These were the indictments carried from one court sitting to another until finally, after enough time had passed, they simply expired. Persistent as all these problems were, colonial courts everywhere in British America had to grapple with them.[11] No precise measure of their impact on law enforcement can be offered here, but it was certainly substantial.

The different causes for dismissals—negligent jurymen, witnesses, and prosecutors; defendants dying or disappearing; lack of evidence—varied in their effect on the criminal process. The record on morals charges is clear. Most resulted in conviction or dismissal. It seems likely that grand jurors, rather than screen morals charges themselves, left that job for the trial court. The extremely low dismissal rate for homicide underscores the deep concern about this offense and the intense interest of witnesses and prosecutors in such cases.

By and large, those crimes generating a high proportion of convictions must have posed a serious threat to the public or private social order. Conversely, crimes with a relatively low conviction rate would have been taken less seriously. Theft, more than any other crime, offers a graphic pattern of outcomes. If the security of private property was a high priority in North Carolina, law enforcers could not achieve it.[12] And the character of the colony effectively explains that. Unlike neighboring colonies to the north, North Carolina remained until the latter part of the eighteenth century a frontier province of few towns and sparse population. This setting offered relatively little worth stealing and relatively little restraint on lawlessness. Law enforcers therefore

9. See General Court, July, 1727, *NCHCR,* VI, 420–22; *Crown v. Davis,* July, 1744, General Court Criminal Papers, 1740–44.

10. See, for example, Pasquotank County Court Reference, New Action, Minute Docket, 1765–71.

11. See, for example, Scott, *Criminal Law in Colonial Virginia,* 68; Greenberg, *Crime and Law Enforcement in New York,* 172–73.

12. This was not the case in the colony of New York. See Greenberg, *Crime and Law Enforcement in New York,* 92.

dealt more firmly with threats to the social order than with threats to property.

While the data show clearly that lawmen handled some crimes more effectively than others, patterns of case dispositions changed with time (Table 14). And it is not difficult to link these changes to shifting circumstances within the colony. Consider the final settlement of morals charges. For a thirty-year period in the eighteenth century, grand juries did not dismiss a single one. While suspects would likely face indictment, the overall rate at which they were convicted declined as time passed. Here we see a phenomenon occurring in North Carolina that

TABLE 14
DISPOSITION OF SELECTED CHARGES, BY DECADE

	Assault		Theft		Morals Crimes		Animal Stealing	
Ignoramus								
1720s	—	—	10	(27.78%)	1	(11.11%)	—	—
1730s	43	(55.12%)	32	(56.14)	—	—	3	(20.00%)
1740s	55	(56.70)	24	(50.00)	—	—	13	(59.09)
1750s	58	(32.95)	11	(33.33)	—	—	4	(36.36)
1760s	127	(32.15)	32	(22.07)	7	(10.07)	26	(37.68)
Convicted								
1720s	2	(25.00)	14	(38.39)	6	(66.66)	2	(100.00)
1730s	16	(20.51)	10	(17.54)	7	(63.63)	5	(33.33)
1740s	25	(25.77)	8	(16.67)	14	(25.45)	3	(13.63)
1750s	71	(40.34)	7	(21.21)	10	(32.25)	2	(18.18)
1760s	208	(52.65)	53	(36.55)	29	(44.61)	19	(27.54)
Acquitted								
1720s	—	—	7	(19.44)	—	—	—	—
1730s	9	(11.53)	3	(5.26)	2	(18.18)	2	(13.33)
1740s	15	(15.46)	7	(14.58)	10	(18.18)	10	(18.18)
1750s	33	(18.75)	13	(39.39)	4	(12.90)	4	(36.36)
1760s	43	(10.88)	47	(32.41)	7	(10.77)	19	(27.54)
Dismissed								
1720s	6	(75.00)	5	(13.89)	2	(22.22)	—	—
1730s	10	(12.82)	12	(21.05)	2	(18.18)	5	(33.33)
1740s	2	(2.06)	9	(18.75)	31	(56.36)	1	(4.55)
1750s	14	(7.95)	2	(6.06)	17	(54.83)	1	(9.09)
1760s	17	(4.30)	13	(8.97)	22	(33.84)	5	(7.24)

has been noted in other colonies as well.[13] Rigid moral codes (never remarkably rigid in North Carolina to begin with) were loosening, and more serious crime, a product of economic and demographic growth, was now demanding the attention of lawmen. Animal theft, for example, became an increasingly irksome property crime, which the assembly recognized by providing harsher punishment for it in 1741 and 1774. When a crime was on the rise, the courts moved to handle it more effectively. In the thirty-year period before the Revolution, grand juries returned a smaller proportion of no bills and trial juries a larger proportion of convictions for animal theft. For other acts of stealing, the courts were not as successful in securing convictions. Yet as time passed, thieves could at least expect a more vigorous response from law enforcers. For assault, however, case outcomes changed dramatically. Within a forty-year period, the conviction rate doubled. This is one more piece of evidence of the special need to control behavior that undermined a stable social order.

While external circumstances could influence the disposition of a case, so could the court that had jurisdiction. Data generated by the General Court and county courts, which operated concurrently until 1754, show that county courts were more likely to indict and convict, and were less likely to dismiss (Table 15). County courts certainly avoided some of the troubles that impaired higher court proceedings. Litigants, for example, did not have to travel long distances to reach the local courts, and prosecutors could collect evidence more easily in a local setting. A comparison of the prosecution record of the Superior Court (from 1760 to 1772) with that of the General Court (to 1754) shows that for assault and theft, and for all other crimes as well, the Superior Court almost consistently demonstrated greater effectiveness in indicting, convicting, and dismissing. Evidence for the lower courts also points to an improving record of case dispositions (Table 16). In fact, the data lead to the inescapable albeit predictable conclusion that law enforcement was more and more competent with time (Table 17). Along with the colony's maturation came a decline in no bills and dismissals, and an increase in convictions. But this kind of positive change did not extend to every aspect of the criminal process. The courts persistently fell short in one area—completing prosecutions (Table 18). The Carolina courts were not hopelessly failing in this area—New York

13. See Flaherty, "Law and the Enforcement of Morals," 61.

TABLE 15
DISPOSITION OF CHARGES, BY COURT, 1670–1776

	Assault		Theft		All Crimes	
Ignoramus						
General	96	(52.45%)	69	(40.35%)	286	(39.94%)
Superior	77	(36.84)	24	(21.81)	201	(27.05)
County	130	(26.10)	27	(25.23)	276	(20.89)
Convicted						
General	39	(21.31)	46	(26.90)	182	(25.41)
Superior	102	(48.80)	45	(40.90)	287	(38.62)
County	279	(56.02)	32	(29.90)	594	(44.96)
Acquitted						
General	28	(15.30)	28	(16.37)	116	(16.20)
Superior	27	(12.91)	30	(27.27)	166	(22.34)
County	49	(9.83)	39	(36.44)	261	(19.75)
Dismissed						
General	20	(10.92)	28	(16.37)	132	(18.43)
Superior	3	(1.43)	11	(10.00)	89	(11,97)
County	40	(8.03)	9	(8.41)	190	(14.38)

TABLE 16
DISPOSITION OF CHARGES, BY COURT AND DECADE

	County Court		Court General (1740s) Superior (1760s)	
Ignoramus				
1740s	19	(14.96%)	113	(47.67%)
1760s	113	(25.74)	178	(26.92)
Convicted				
1740s	46	(36.22)	41	(17.29)
1760s	220	(50.11)	255	(38.57)
Acquitted				
1740s	34	(26.77)	72	(16.40)
1760s	72	(16.40)	139	(21.02)
Dismissed				
1740s	28	(22.04)	34	(7.74)
1760s	34	(7.74)	89	(13.46)

TABLE 17
DISPOSITION OF ALL CHARGES WITH KNOWN OUTCOMES, BY DECADE

Decade	Total	Ignoramus	Convicted	Acquitted	Dismissed
1720s	127	29 (22.83%)	41 (32.28%)	17 (13.38%)	40 (31.49%)
1730s	254	125 (49.21)	61 (24.01)	29 (11.41)	39 (15.35)
1740s	367	132 (35.96)	90 (24.52)	78 (21.25)	67 (18.25)
1750s	457	119 (26.03)	166 (36.32)	114 (24.97)	58 (12.69)
1760s	1,136	291 (25.61)	483 (42.51)	211 (18.57)	151 (13.29)
Total	2,341	696 (29.73)	841 (35.92)	449 (19.17)	355 (15.16)

TABLE 18

DISPOSITION OF ALL CHARGES, BY DECADE

Decade	Total	Ignoramus	Convicted	Acquitted	Dismissed	Unknown
1720s	187	29 (15.50%)	41 (21.92%)	17 (9.09%)	40 (21.39%)	60 (32.08%)
1730s	398	125 (31.40)	61 (15.32)	29 (7.28)	39 (9.79)	144 (36.18)
1740s	545	132 (24.22)	90 (16.51)	78 (14.31)	67 (12.29)	178 (32.66)
1750s	673	119 (17.68)	166 (24.66)	114 (16.93)	58 (8.61)	216 (32.09)
1760s	1,591	291 (18.29)	483 (30.35)	211 (13.26)	151 (9.49)	455 (28.59)
Total	3,394	696 (20.50)	841 (24.77)	449 (13.22)	355 (10.45)	1,053 (31.02)

courts, for example, did not resolve 36 percent of their cases.[14] At the least, the Carolina data hint at an improving trend.

How profoundly did biases of class and gender extend into the criminal justice process? Take the example of class (Table 19). Here there is no question that laborers, among the accused identifiable by status, were most likely to be indicted and convicted. Conversely, grand juries returned no bills for planters in greater proportions than for laborers, and trial juries convicted planters in smaller proportions. The simplest explanation would be that the courts prosecuted men of little or no property for the crimes that were easier to convict. But this was not the case. When four common crimes—assault, theft, animal stealing, and homicide—are considered, laborers were convicted 34 of 93 times, a rate of 36.5 percent, and planters 49 of 222 times, a rate of 22 percent. Had planters been convicted for each crime at the same rates as were laborers, there would have been 74.4 planter convictions instead of 49. Conversely, had laborers been convicted for their crimes at the same rate as were planters, there would have been 17.6 laborer convictions instead of 34.[15] Unquestionably, laborers could expect harsher judgments from the courts than could planters. In early Massachusetts, too, the courts favored men of means accused of crimes.[16] But a somewhat different picture emerges when status is linked with the disposition of individual offenses (Table 20). For two crimes in particular, theft and animal stealing, the courts showed a bias against laborers. But for assault, the data reveal a pronounced bias against planters. Judged by men of property, laborers accused of property crimes could expect an unfavorable outcome. The courts tolerated crimes of violence among the poor but took those same acts by planters more seriously.

14. Greenberg, *Crime and Law Enforcement in New York*, 190.
15. The calculations were as follows:

	Assault Conv. Total	Theft Conv. Total	Murder Conv. Total	An. St. Conv. Total
Planters	32 120	9 55	5 15	3 32
Laborers	7 30	16 32	4 6	7 25

If planters were convicted in the same proportion as were laborers for each crime, the number of convicted planters would be $7 \div 30 \times 120 \;+\; 16 \div 32 \times 55 \;+\; 4 \div 6 \times 15 \;+\; 7 \div 25 \times 32 = 74.46$. Reversing to obtain the number of convicted laborers yields $32 \div 120 \times 30 \;+\; 9 \div 55 \times 32 \;+\; 5 \div 15 \times 6 \;+\; 3 \div 32 \times 25 = 17.58$.

16. Faber, "Puritan Criminals," 114.

TABLE 19

DISPOSITION OF CHARGES WITH KNOWN OUTCOMES, BY
SOCIOECONOMIC STATUS, 1663–1776

Classification	Number	Ignoramus	Convicted	Acquitted	Dismissed
Planter	329	47.41%	25.83%	16.10%	10.63%
Laborer	126	37.30	35.71	15.07	11.90
Gentleman	59	45.76	28.81	13.56	11.85
Artisan	41	41.46	34.15	14.63	9.76
Mariner	23	69.57	4.35	17.39	8.70
Overall[1]	735	42.17	31.15	16.19	10.47

[1]Includes all other accused whose status is known and whose case disposition is known.

TABLE 20

DISPOSITION OF SELECTED CHARGES FOR PLANTERS AND LABORERS,
1663–1776

	Assault		Theft		Animal Stealing	
Ignoramus						
Planter	69	(57.50%)	26	(47.27%)	20	(62.50%)
Laborer	6	(50.00)	8	(25.00)	9	(36.00)
Overall	323	(33.89)	129	(31.00)	55	(30.21)
Convicted						
Planter	32	(26.67)	9	(16.36)	3	(9.38)
Laborer	7	(23.33)	16	(50.00)	7	(28.00)
Overall	440	(46.16)	134	(32.21)	48	(26.37)
Acquitted						
Planter	12	(10.00)	15	(27.27)	8	(25.00)
Laborer	3	(10.00)	3	(9.37)	8	(32.00)
Overall	122	(12.80)	104	(25.00)	54	(29.67)
Dismissed						
Planter	7	(5.83)	5	(9.09)	1	(3.12)
Laborer	5	(16.66)	5	(15.62)	1	(4.00)
Overall	68	(7.13)	49	(11.77)	25	(13.73)

The passage of time had a visible impact on those variables, however subtle, that influenced the findings of the courts (Table 21). The data are sparse indeed, but they show that until the 1760s, laborers were indicted and convicted in larger proportions than were planters, though the discrepancy nearly disappeared in the decade before the Revolution. The hint here is that more sophisticated courts were showing less bias than had the courts in earlier years. But this tentative conclusion can be verified only by a study of verdict patterns in the post-Revolutionary era.

If Carolina law enforcers were not always status blind, did they also make distinctions based on sex? Overall, there were only small differences in conviction and acquittal rates for men and women (Table 22). Such was also the case in early New York and Massachusetts, two colonies for which comparative data are available.[17] Yet both these colonies show a slightly higher male conviction rate, while North Carolina's is slightly lower. The statistics equivocate on whether the courts treated women more favorably than men, a position that few recent studies support.[18] On closer inspection, the Carolina data reveal no such leniency. When verdicts for four different crimes are combined, men were convicted 586 of 1,440 times, a rate of 40.7 percent, and women 67 of 171 times, a rate of 39.2 percent. Had men been convicted for each crime at the same rate as were women, there would have been 600.9 male convictions instead of 586. Conversely, had women been convicted of their crimes at the same rate as men, there would have been 63.2 female convictions instead of 67.[19] If anything, the Carolina

17. The figures for New York are 48.1 percent male and 46.5 percent female (Greenberg, *Crime and Law Enforcement in New York,* 77), and for Massachusetts are 45.8 percent male and 39.9 percent female (Hull, "Female Felons," 151–52).

18. See Samaha, *Law and Order in Historical Perspective,* 57; Beattie, "Crime and the Courts in Surrey," in Cockburn (ed.), *Crime in England,* 182–83; Carol Z. Wiener, "Sex-Roles and Crime in Late Elizabethan Hertfordshire," *Journal of Social History,* VIII (1975), 39; Greenberg, *Crime and Law Enforcement in New York,* 77–78; and Hoffer and Scott (eds.), *Criminal Proceedings in Colonial Virginia,* lxix.

19. The figures are:

	Assault Conv. Total		Theft Conv. Total		Homicide Conv. Total		Ad./For Conv. Total	
Men	413	899	119	367	21	78	33	96
Women	27	56	15	48	2	15	23	52

experience points to *harsher* treatment for women. But, once again, this is a general statement that will not always hold up when considered in light of individual offenses. In fact, a defendant's gender could be relevant to the disposition of a case, depending on the charge. For some crimes, the Carolina courts treated women differently because of their sex or because of the gender-related aspects of the crime; and for other crimes, the courts treated women and men the same way.

Gender played an obvious role in how courts dealt with moral misbehavior. Women accused of adultery, fornication, or bastardy faced a much higher conviction rate and lower acquittal rate than did their male counterparts. Women apparently had the same experience in Massachusetts and in the southern colonies as well.[20] In North Carolina the male conviction rate for adultery was 16.1 percent and the female rate was 29.7.[21] For this offense, judicial bias was, in a sense, already built into the legal system. As the law of adultery was written, it recognized greater culpability on the woman's part. A married man was an adulterer only if his partner in crime was married. A woman having an extramarital affair was always an adulteress—her partner's marital status was irrelevant.[22] When it came to morals crimes and gender, the records depict a double standard in the Carolina colony that demanded a stricter code of morality from women than from men. Herein lies an affirmation of women as the mainstay of morality. Those who resisted this role challenged an array of entrenched attitudes about motherhood, wifely behavior, and the family. Their high conviction rates show that they were dealt with accordingly.

The number of convicted men would be $27 \div 56 \times 899 \ + \ 15 \div 48 \times 367 \ + \ 2 \div 15 \times 78 \ + \ 23 \div 52 \times 96 = 601.00$. The number of convicted women would be $413 \div 899 \times 56 \ + \ 119 \div 367 \times 48 \ + \ 21 \div 78 \times 15 \ + \ 33 \div 96 \times 52 = 63.20$.

20. According to Estelle Brenda Freedman ("Their Sisters' Keepers: The Origins of Female Corrections in America" [Ph.D. dissertation, Columbia University, 1976], in colonial Massachusetts "a far larger proportion of the women had convictions for fornication or lascivious behavior than did men" (p. 7). Spruill (*Women's Life and Work in the Southern Colonies*) states that "female offenders against morality [in the southern colonies] usually fared worse than male defendants" (p. 339). A study of female criminals in Washington, D.C., in the 1970s shows that "for offenses related to prostitution . . . women are much less likely to have their cases dismissed than are men" (Simon and Sharma, "The Female Defendant," Sec. IV, p. 9).

21. Between the years 1663 and 1776, there were eighty-seven men and thirty-seven women charged with adultery. Of these, fourteen men and eleven women were convicted.

22. See John Demos, *A Little Commonwealth: Family Life in Plymouth Colony* (New York, 1970), 97; and Flaherty, "Law and the Enforcement of Morals," 55.

TABLE 21

DISPOSITION OF CHARGES FOR PLANTERS AND LABORERS, BY DECADE

Decade	Ignoramus				Convicted				Acquitted				Dismissed			
	P		L		P		L		P		L		P		L	
1720s	3	(12.50%)	2	(16.66%)	10	(41.66%)	8	(66.67%)	1	(4.17%)	1	(8.33%)	10	(41.66%)	1	(8.33%)
1730s	50	(56.81)	15	(46.87)	21	(23.86)	8	(25.00)	6	(6.81)	4	(12.50)	11	(12.50)	5	(15.62)
1740s	58	(53.21)	3	(17.65)	18	(16.51)	7	(41.18)	22	(20.18)	5	(29.41)	11	(10.09)	2	(11.76)
1750s	14	(70.00)	2	(33.33)	4	(20.00)	3	(50.00)	1	(5.00)	1	(16.66)	1	(5.00)	—	—
1760s	23	(45.09)	20	(42.55)	20	(39.22)	15	(31.91)	8	(15.69)	8	(17.02)	—	—	4	(8.51)

TABLE 22
DISPOSITION OF SELECTED CHARGES FOR MEN AND WOMEN, 1663–1776

Charge	Ignoramus		Convicted		Acquitted		Dismissed	
	M	F	M	F	M	F	M	F
Assault	306 (34.15%)	16 (28.57%)	413 (46.09%)	27 (48.21%)	114 (12.72%)	8 (14.29%)	63 (7.03%)	5 (8.92%)
Theft	111 (30.41)	16 (33.33)	119 (32.60)	15 (31.25)	96 (26.30)	8 (16.67)	39 (10.68)	9 (18.75)
Homicide	19 (30.64)	6 (40.00)	21 (33.87)	2 (13.33)	20 (32.25)	7 (46.67)	2 (3.22)	—
Adult./forn./ bast.	3 (2.97)	2 (2.85)	39 (38.61)	34 (48.57)	16 (15.84)	6 (8.57)	43 (42.57)	28 (40.00)
Other crimes	329 (24.84)	24 (32.00)	452 (34.13)	25 (33.33)	317 (23.94)	17 (22.66)	226 (17.06)	9 (12.00)
All crimes	768 (27.94)	64 (24.24)	1,044 (37.99)	103 (39.01)	563 (20.48)	46 (17.42)	373 (13.57)	51 (19.31)

Gender also influenced the findings of the courts in cases of homicide. Female murder convictions occurred at a lower rate than did those for males, and acquittals were at a higher rate. Yet a large proportion of killings allegedly committed by women involved the same kind of victim—an infant. Guilty verdicts for infanticide were rare in North Carolina, as they were in other colonies, such as Maryland and Massachusetts, for which data are available.[23] Consider, for example, a young woman in court, accused of murdering her baby. The trial jury would weigh the evidence, dubious at best, the defendant's credibility, and the circumstances surrounding the act. None of these variables were directly relevant to gender. Instead, the comparatively large proportion of acquittals for women accused of homicide reflects not a judicial leniency toward women but a particular response to the nature of the crime and the near impossibility of proving it.

If gender did play a role, albeit a different one in the disposition of crimes such as adultery and homicide, it had no significant role at all in cases of assault and theft. Women who threatened the social order or put private property in jeopardy had stepped out of their female world and had entered the world of men. Once this occurred, their gender made no difference. Ironic as it may be, women were subordinate to men, but once they stole or physically hurt someone, they were treated just the same.

If there is any crime that speaks in the records through its silence, it is rape. Only nine cases involving an accused white male were recorded for the entire colonial period. Seven of these cases have a known outcome. Four ended in no bills, two in acquittals, and one in dismissal. Studies of early Virginia and South Carolina have found this same low incidence of reported rape and low rate of conviction.[24] If we assume that rape occurred more than nine times in North Carolina, its absence from the records is a commentary on social attitudes toward the sexual assault of women. Admittedly, the stigma against bringing a rape charge was substantial. But the improbably small number of prosecutions and the failure to convict nearly all those accused indicate that Carolina society

23. Semmes, *Crime and Punishment in Early Maryland,* 128; Hoffer and Hull, *Murdering Mothers,* 74. Acquittals for infanticide were also common in eighteenth-century English courts. See Beattie, "The Criminality of Women," 84.

24. Rankin, *Criminal Trial Proceedings in Virginia,* 220–22; Michael S. Hindus, "The Social Context of Crime in Massachusetts and South Carolina, 1760–1783: Theoretical and Quantitative Perspectives," Newberry Papers in Family and Community History (1975), Table 1.

did not take this offense seriously. Without inferring too much from the data, we can say that the criminal record on rape gives more apparent credence to an eighteenth-century belief in female prurience. Not surprisingly, a somewhat different story could be told if the alleged rapist was black. While rape of a white woman, regardless of the race of the rapist, was a capital crime, there was not a single recorded white conviction, but six convictions of slaves. Evidence from the records makes clear that in cases of rape, justices and slaveowners convicted on the testimony of a single witness—the white victim. Consider the case of Harry, convicted of raping sixteen-year-old Mary Busby. According to her testimony, he committed the rape "by entering her Body by force and against her Will . . . & Emitted his Seed." In 1775, Christianna Atwater swore to a freeholders court in New Bern that the slave Ben "on the night of the Sixteenth of August last Committed or Endeavored to Commit a Rape upon [her]."[25] The obvious difference in the outcome of rape trials for slaves and whites hints at a host of sexual undertones. It also highlights white attitudes toward Negro sexuality and all the anxieties and insecurities these attitudes reflected. A white woman raped by a slave was no longer a seductress; she was the victim of black sexual aggression.

With the passage of time, conviction rates for men and women changed (Table 23). From the 1730s through the 1750s, trial juries continued to find guilty a larger proportion of accused women than men. But as the colony matured, the difference narrowed until finally, on the eve of the Revolution, the courts convicted men at a higher rate. It could be that by mid-century, women began engaging in what had been largely male crime. Or the decline in morals prosecutions, which typically ended in a higher rate of female conviction, may account for the more comparable male/female conviction rates later in the century. While neither explanation is evident in the data, it is clear that when women committed crimes, they were treated more and more like men.

Oddly enough, the county where a prosecution occurred had a discernible impact on the outcome of cases for men and women (Table 24). In Hyde County, along Pamlico Sound, for example, the male conviction rate was very high relative to the rate for females, and the female acquittal rate comparatively low. Conversely, in Bertie, an old north-

25. *Crown* v. *Harry,* July, 1740, Secretary of State, Court Records, Magistrates and Freeholders Courts; *Crown* v. *Ben,* September, 1775, Treasurer and Comptroller, Miscellaneous Group, 1738–1909.

TABLE 23
DISPOSITION OF CHARGES, FOR MEN AND WOMEN, BY DECADE

Decade	Ignoramus		Convicted		Acquitted		Dismissed	
	M	F	M	F	M	F	M	F
1720s	24 (22.64%)	5 (23.81%)	32 (30.18%)	9 (42.86%)	12 (11.32%)	5 (23.81%)	38 (35.84%)	2 (9.52%)
1730s	111 (49.33)	12 (54.55)	55 (24.44)	6 (27.27)	27 (12.00)	2 (9.09)	32 (14.22)	2 (9.09%)
1740s	125 (38.81)	6 (14.63)	72 (22.36)	15 (36.59)	73 (22.67)	5 (12.19)	52 (16.14)	15 (36.59)
1750s	112 (27.65)	6 (13.95)	145 (35.80)	16 (37.21)	101 (24.93)	10 (23.26)	47 (11.60)	11 (25.58)
1760s	270 (25.98)	21 (23.59)	440 (42.34)	35 (39.32)	197 (18.96)	14 (15.73)	132 (12.70)	19 (21.34)

TABLE 24

DISPOSITION OF CHARGES, FOR MEN AND WOMEN, BY COUNTY, 1663–1776

	Chowan	Bertie	Onslow	Hyde	Tyrrell	Rowan
Ignoramus						
Male	55 (35.48%)	77 (35.00%)	64 (25.00%)	55 (35.03%)	56 (41.48%)	52 (27.22%)
Female	3 (18.75)	6 (20.00)	4 (18.18)	12 (50.00)	3 (33.33)	2 (22.22)
Convicted						
Male	53 (34.19)	56 (25.45)	139 (54.29)	63 (40.13)	45 (33.33)	91 (47.64)
Female	6 (37.50)	10 (33.33)	12 (54.54)	7 (29.17)	3 (33.33)	4 (44.44)
Acquitted						
Male	26 (16.70)	48 (21.81)	36 (14.06)	16 (10.19)	23 (17.03)	27 (14.13)
Female	3 (18.75)	1 (3.33)	5 (22.72)	1 (4.17)	1 (11.11)	3 (33.33)
Dismissed						
Male	21 (13.54)	39 (17.72)	17 (6.64)	23 (14.65)	11 (8.14)	21 (10.99)
Female	4 (25.00)	13 (43.33)	1 (4.54)	4 (16.66)	2 (22.22)	— —

eastern county, men were less likely to be convicted and much more likely to be acquitted. At the same time, male/female conviction rates are strikingly similar for four of these six counties. As scarce as the data are for this kind of analysis, it seems virtually impossible to explain apparent links between gender and the crime site. Economic and social conditions, as well as the abilities or biases of lawmen, were no doubt influential where differences occurred.

If location played an equivocal role in the disposition of male and female crime, so did the court itself (Table 25). Data for the General Court, which provide the largest sample for the higher courts, show the female conviction rate to be notably higher than that for males. For the other courts, including those of the counties, male and female conviction rates scarcely differed. Once again, the lack of data makes it difficult to interpret these figures with any precision. Yet women charged with lesser crimes seemed to fare slightly better than did men, and in the higher courts, where they were accused of more serious offenses, they fared better than did men in the later years.

The disposition of slave crime has to be placed in an entirely separate category of crime control. Just the wording of the statute law alone indicates clearly that the odds were weighted, and purposefully so, against slave men and slave women accused of crimes. A law of 1715, for

TABLE 25

DISPOSITION OF CHARGES, FOR MEN AND WOMEN, BY COURT, 1670–1776

	General Court		Supreme Court		Superior Court		County Court	
Ignoramus								
Male	259	(38.03%)	45	(36.88%)	188	(26.55%)	252	(21.35%)
Female	25	(31.65)	3	(33.33)	13	(33.33)	23	(16.91)
Convicted								
Male	186	(27.31)	30	(24.59)	273	(38.55)	534	(45.25)
Female	28	(35.44)	2	(22.22)	14	(35.90)	59	(43.38)
Acquitted								
Male	119	(17.47)	40	(32.78)	157	(22.17)	239	(20.25)
Female	15	(18.99)	2	(22.22)	9	(23.08)	19	(13.97)
Dismissed								
Male	117	(17.18)	7	(5.73)	90	(12.71)	155	(13.13)
Female	11	(13.92)	2	(22.22)	3	(7.69)	35	(25.73)

example, required a slave "guilty of any Crime or Offence" to be tried by a freeholders court. A 1741 statute provided that suspected slave felons be judged in the same way and, "being then found guilty," pay the considerable penalty. Thus, written into the formal law was a presumption of guilt. Indeed, the extant slave court records, some of which list witnesses in detail, show that all testified against the accused slave and none for. That was, after all, what the slave system required. There also could be no delay in the trial of slave suspects. In fact, a glance at a few freeholders court records shows that the wheels of justice could turn amazingly fast. On February 22, 1741, a Pasquotank County court convicted Scipio of a theft committed four days earlier. In 1748 a Beaufort court quickly found slaves Jack and Stephen guilty of jail escape and theft, less than a week after the crime occurred.[26] Slaves were scarcely ever confined to jail, where they then became absent workers. Suspected of crimes, they had behaved so repugnantly and dangerously to the white world and to their own bondage, informal punishment by their own masters could not be adequate. Their prosecution had to be public and sufficiently chilling to terrorize other potential resisters. Conventional English law could not secure these objectives, nor could a conventional jury trial. While a group of white judges used its "best Judgment & Discretion," as the law euphemistically put it, a slave court trial was a judgment on the gravity of the crime.

Since ordinary felony trial rules did not apply to accused slaves and since the law is vague about procedure, we must speculate how these summary courts reached a verdict. Slaves probably could not subpoena or cross-examine witnesses, though information from "credible Witnesses" or "Negroes, Mulattoes or Indians," slave or free, could be offered on their behalf. Yet there is virtually no evidence of this. Nor is there evidence that, as the law provided, a master or overseer would "appear at the Tryal and make what just Defence he can." Slaves could, like their white counterparts, plead not guilty, as did Jem to the charge of raping Sarah Langly and Rose to the charge of arson, but such pleas were to no avail.[27] The thrust of a slave court trial was to prove a presumption of guilt. After all, accused slaves had ventured far beyond a

26. Acts of 1715, 1741, *NCSR*, XXIII, 64, 202; *Crown* v. *Scipio*, February, 1741, and *Crown* v. *Jack and Stephen*, December, 1748, Secretary of State, Court Records, Magistrates and Freeholders Courts.

27. *Crown* v. *Jem*, April, 1775, New Bern District Court Miscellaneous Records, 1758–1806; *Crown* v. *Rose*, n.d., Halifax District Court Miscellaneous Records, 1763–1808.

level of tolerable resistance, and from the perspective of whites, slavery could not survive without a formal process for judgment and punishment. But this was still a world of English men and women, rational and humane. This was still a world in which certain rights had to be respected, to separate man from beast. Hence the necessity for pretense.

Early criminal justice had a blind side when it came to slaves, because English rules of law could not sustain human bondage. A certain amount of bias also filtered into the system when it dealt with whites. A different standard of justice, for example, applied at times to men of different status. In the case of property crimes, the courts favored men of means. A different standard of justice also applied to women *if* they were accused of morals crimes. These findings underscore and confirm the critical role of race in criminal justice and the important roles of class and gender. Far from being blind to such variables, the courts observed them closely. Admittedly, in the regular courts their influence was more subtle, but in the arena of the freeholders courts, there was no place for subtlety.

Beyond the specific elements of race, status, and gender, patterns of criminal prosecutions provide some further insight into the Carolina world. The courts prosecuted most effectively those offenses that threatened social cohesion—the assaults, contempts, and homicides. At least in intent, this made North Carolina much like colonies to the north.[28] The record on property crimes was not nearly as impressive, though it improved with the passage of time. Here, the pattern is predictable. As North Carolina matured, as urban areas developed and society became more complex, theft figured more importantly in the range of crimes prosecuted by the courts and was taken far more seriously. No offense more effectively highlighted social and religious attitudes than did crimes against morality. Prosecutions for adultery, swearing, fornication, etc., declined over time, showing clearly the growing secularism of early Carolina.

As North Carolina matured, in both physical and temporal ways, so did its legal institutions change. As time passed, the overall proportion of convictions increased, but the proportion of unknown outcomes did not significantly decline. The hint, however tenuous, is of the courts'

28. See Edmund S. Morgan, *The Puritan Family: Religion and Domestic Relations in Seventeenth-Century New England* (New York, 1944), 17; and Michael Zuckerman, *Peaceable Kingdoms: New England Towns in the Eighteenth Century* (New York, 1970), 64–65.

growing ability to do their job. At the same time, the courts could not come to grips with the vexing problem of bringing all cases to completion. Compressing the evidence makes it possible to see that the lower courts performed more effectively than did the higher courts. Despite the rather unsavory reputation of justices of the peace, the criminal courts they presided over produced comparatively creditable results. This is not to say that the higher courts failed when their counterparts at the lower level succeeded. The Superior Court, for example, the last of the colonial higher courts, achieved a much higher rate of conviction than had the General Court. At the same time, it managed to bring cases to trial, on the average, more quickly than had its predecessor.[29] Indeed, criminal justice practices at every level improved with time, but the county courts, long the bedrock of local government, maintained overall a more impressive record.

29. This finding is based on 103 General Court observations showing the median number of days from date of crime to court as ninety-one, and on 129 Superior Court observations showing the median number of days as sixty.

VI

PUNISHMENT

[M]ade his Exit at the Gallows
—North Carolina Gazette, *July 14, 1775*

In the eighteenth century, punishment had a single purpose—"to deter men from offending."[1] Criminal sanctions were not intended to rehabilitate offenders or to make them repent. Indeed, all men and women were sinners, and those who violated the law had, at a time of weakness, failed to control their baser instincts. Penal measures would discourage them from misbehaving again or discourage others from following their example.

In theory, meting out punishment was not an arbitrary exercise. Both legislation and the common law established a criminal code that defined criminal acts and sanctions. The formal law made punishment appropriate to the seriousness of the offense, measured by its threat to "the public safety and happiness." In actual practice, the punishment dictated by English and American courts was not always consistent with what the law required.[2] Here, judges could exercise discretion in the sanctions they imposed, and jurors could downgrade an offense to mitigate the penalty. Both practices reflected contemporary perceptions about crime and criminals. A theft motivated by poverty, for example, was "far more worthy of compassion, than when committed through avarice." A spontaneous killing was "less penal" than one carried out with "cool deliberate malice." Violators of the law might be mere offenders—those who showed a lack of control over wicked impulses.

1. Blackstone, *Commentaries,* IV, 10.
2. *Ibid.*, 16; Kathryn Preyer, "Penal Measures in the American Colonies: An Overview," *AJLH,* XXVI (1982), 334; Beattie, "Crime and the Courts in Surrey," in Cockburn (ed.), *Crime in England,* 174–86; Herrup, "Law and Morality," 102–23.

Or they might be actual criminals—those who completely surrendered to such impulses. A certain amount of discretion in criminal sanctions allowed the courts to adjust penalties according to the gravity of the crime and the reputation of the convicted. Statute and common law set certain boundaries, but the courts also considered "the Baseness, Enormity, and dangerouss Tendency of [the crime], the malice, Deliberation and Wilfulness, or the Inconsideration, Suddenness and Surprize with which it was committed, the Age, Quality and Degree of the Offender, and all other Circumstances which may any way aggravate or extenuate the Guilt."[3]

Much like those in other colonies, North Carolina's criminal code was a limited one. Legislation on crime and penalties dealt chiefly with moral misbehavior, the activities of servants and slaves, and a few specific offenses that demanded special attention because of their prevalence. Until 1749, substantive law provided that "the laws of England" were to be "the Laws" of the colony "so far as they are compatible with our way of living." In that year, the assembly recognized some two hundred English statutes relating to law enforcement that, according to their usefulness and practicality, would be observed in the colony. These statutes dealt with misdeeds ranging from rape to murder to counterfeiting. Suffice it to say that the Carolina courts, still operating in something of a wilderness, paid scant attention to this lengthy list of English laws. Instead, the colonial courts imposed "traditional" English punishments along with their own. Carolina men and women who broke the law were fined, whipped, pilloried, carted, humiliated with labels, and executed. A very few were banished, even fewer imprisoned. One sanction popular in England after 1717—transportation—was rarely imposed anywhere in America.[4]

English law allowed judges the greatest latitude in punishing misdemeanors, with the exception of crimes against morality. This careful regulation of public morality mirrored English attitudes, which worked their considerable influence on colonial Americans. North Carolina's early preoccupation with sin as crime, especially in the absence of force-

3. Blackstone, *Commentaries,* IV, 15; Herrup, "Law and Morality," 110; Hawkins, *A Treatise of the Pleas of the Crown,* II, 445.

4. Act of 1711, *NCSR,* XXV, 153; act of 1749, *NCSR,* XXIII, 317; Preyer, "Penal Measures in the American Colonies," 330; Goebel and Naughton, *Law Enforcement in Colonial New York,* 704–10. On transportation, see Beattie, "Crime and the Courts in Surrey," in Cockburn (ed.), *Crime in England,* 158.

ful religious institutions, also reflected the dearth of more serious crime in the colony. In 1715, legislators produced a statute that copiously detailed immoral acts and their punishment. The typical fine for swearing was set at 2s. 6d. "for every Oath or Curse" and increased to 5s. for a "person in Office." To regulate "the odious & loathsome Sin of Drunkenness," inebriates would pay 5s., and Sabbath offenders 10s. Men and women who could not pay the fine would spend three hours in the stocks. Swearing and drunkenness may have upset the moral order, but the hefty fines for sex-related sins indicated that these were far more serious offenses. Fornicators paid 50s., adulterers £5. The alternative was to be "publickly whipped at the Discretion of the Court, not exceeding One and twenty lashes." If these sex-related offenses produced a child, and the mother refused to name the father, or the father refused to maintain the child, both were subject to "Corporal or other punishment."[5] In 1741, perhaps in response to the emergence of more serious crime or, more likely, to changing values, the assembly reduced by half the penalties for drunkenness and fornication. Legislators also altered the punishment for bastardy so as to give parents a more compelling reason to support their child. Now negligent offenders could be "committed to Prison" until they provided for their offspring.[6]

In actual practice, when it came to morals crimes, there was much variation in sentencing. An early adultery case, for example, resulted in a penalty consistent with the letter of the law when the General Court fined John Hassell £5 for cohabiting with Sarah Wilkinson "in a Lew'd and Dishonest manner." But adulterers in later years found themselves, for the most part, at the mercy of the bench. In 1740 a Pasquotank County court fined an adulterous couple £15, exceedingly more than the law required. In 1755, Rebecca Lewis and Richard Thomas, convicted of adultery, received a sentence of just 1s. each. So did adulterer John Brooks two years later. In 1768 a Halifax County court fined two adulterous couples one penny each, but a year later the same court imposed a 25s. fine on William Jackson and Lucretia Goodwin for abandoning their spouses for each other.[7] Swearers also found that

5. Act of 1715, *NCSR*, XXIII, 3–6.
6. Act of 1741, *ibid.*, 173–74.
7. *Crown* v. *Hassell*, March, 1721, *NCHCR*, V, 242; *Crown* v. *Martin and Cartwright*, January, 1740, Pasquotank County Court Minutes, April, 1737–July, 1753; *Crown* v. *Thomas and Lewis*, November, 1755, Edgecombe County Court Crown Docket, 1755–56; *Crown* v. *Brooks*, March, 1757, Beaufort County Court Appearance, Prosecution, and Reference Dockets, 1756–61, 1756–58; *Crown* v. *Jarrell and Hill*, May,

judges deviated from the statute law. In 1748, Mathew Huggins was fined not the prescribed 2s. 6d., but 1s. instead. Whatever profanity it was that brought six men into an Onslow County court in 1764 the records do not say, but each offender was penalized 5s. Three swearers fared better at a Halifax County court in 1769 when the bench set their fine at one penny each.[8] Even fornicators, whose behavior threatened the state with a child to support, received sentences nowhere near what the law required. In 1747 a Bertie County court mercifully fined Elizabeth Findlay and John Wotsford 1s. each instead of the required 25. Another unmarried couple were equally fortunate in 1768 to pay an even smaller penalty of one penny. Here the records say time and again that judges ignored the statute law, in most cases to mitigate the punishment, for men and women convicted of morals crimes. Despite the heavy fines prescribed by law, most offenders received little more than a slap on the wrist. But there are cases on record in which the fine was heavy: 25s. for fornication, £10 for adultery.[9] Special circumstances no doubt explain the harsher price—a remorseless offender, a repeater, or a bench that, for whatever reason, took a particular morals crime most seriously.

For other misdemeanors, Carolina judges were, like their English counterparts, allowed by law a large measure of discretion in sentencing. A law enacted in 1711 in response to the Cary Rebellion and renewed in 1715 penalized contempt, sedition, "Conspiracys, Riotts or any manner of unlawful Feuds" by "fine, imprisonment or otherwise at the discretion of the Justices of the General Court." For assault and jail escape, North Carolina justices followed the English practice of imposing fines and terms in jail. With so much allowable discretion, it is obvious why sentences varied greatly. In most cases, judicial logic remains a mystery. At times, for example, the same bench prescribed different penalties for people convicted of the same crime. Mathew

---

1769, and Crown v. Crowley and Jones, August, 1769, Halifax County Court Crown Docket, 1759–70; Crown v. Jackson and Crown v. Goodwin, August, 1770, Halifax County Court Crown Docket, 1759–70.

8. Crown v. Huggins, March, 1748, General Court Dockets, 1748–52. See September, 1764, Onslow County Court Crown Docket, 1763–66, 1769, in Halifax County Court Crown Docket, 1759–70.

9. Crown v. Findlay and Wotsford, May, 1747, Bertie County Court Miscellaneous Dockets, 1725–90; Crown v. Sparks and Fawcett, August, 1768, Halifax County Court Crown Docket, 1759–70; Crown v. Simpson, March, 1723, NCHCR, V, 346; Crown v. Catholick, June, 1766, Onslow County Court Crown Docket, 1766–74.

Raiford and William Coleman were each convicted of assaulting a justice of the peace. Raiford paid 20s.; Coleman, 10s. During a two-day session in June, 1768, the Wilmington District Court heard six assault cases, fining four of the offenders 1s. each, and the others 5s. and £10, respectively.[10] Silent as usual about the discrepancy, the records would, if they could, likely link a more serious assault with a heftier fine. Indeed, courts more consistent in their punishments may have been less sensitive to degrees of difference among the same crimes. As confusing as the data are, a pattern of leniency or harshness emerges, depending on the court. From 1754 to 1755, most assault offenders in a Hyde County court received nothing worse than a 1s. fine. That was also the favorite penalty for trespass at a higher court session in 1761, but the same court required a payment of £5 from five men convicted of assault.[11]

Nearly all justices uniformly tried to avoid sentencing offenders to jail. Only a very few of these penalties appear anywhere in the records. Margaret Carter, for example, convicted of stealing 9d. worth of goods, was ordered to spend six months in jail. So was Barny Jones, for an unnamed offense, and so was Isaiah Jones, for burning a "tar kiln."[12] If, as in most colonies, jails were rarely used, it was because they were rarely suited to long confinements.[13] Jails, as such, did not even exist in North Carolina before the early eighteenth century. Thus a court could sentence an offender to prison when an adequate one did not exist. In 1698 the General Court prescribed a year's confinement to forgerer Stephen Manwaring, only to have him threaten "the blood and lives of the Honorable members of this Court . . . [because] there is not any Close prison to secure him in." In 1715 the assembly ordered the none-too-happy provost marshal to use his own house as "the County prison until

10. Baker, "Criminal Courts and Procedure at Common Law," in Cockburn (ed.), *Crime in England,* 43; act of 1711, *NCSR,* XXV, 152; act of 1715, *NCSR,* XXIII, 38–39; Davis, *Justice of Peace,* 17, 156; *Crown v. Raiford* and *Crown v. Coleman,* March, 1762, Salisbury District Court Criminal Action Papers, 1760–71, and Salisbury District Court Trial and Minute Docket, 1761–90. See Wilmington District Court Minutes, Superior Court, 1760–83.

11. See Hyde County Court Appearance, Crown, Reference, and Prosecution Dockets, 1744–61; and New Bern District Court Trial, Argument, Reference, and Appearance Docket, 1758–60.

12. *Crown v. Carter,* June, 1756, Salisbury District Court Minutes, Superior Court, 1756–70; *Crown v. B. Jones,* April, 1762, and *Crown v. I. Jones,* April, 1764, Wilmington District Court Minutes, Superior Court, 1760–83.

13. See Greenberg, *Crime and Law Enforcement in New York,* 125; Powers, *Crime and Punishment in Early Massachusetts,* 234–35; and Preyer, "Penal Measures in the American Colonies," 329.

sufficient Gaols are built." But the counties did not rush to provide them. In 1732 a Bertie County court ordered the marshal to find "some Carpenter to Repair the Gaol of this Precinct & to provide Locks Nails & c. for that purpose." Officials of other counties were charged with "keeping a bad prison."[14] Finally in 1741 the legislature empowered the counties to levy a tax for the construction of "Prisons and Stocks." Carteret County prepared to build a jail of sawed logs no less than four inches thick with a "Strong Double Door . . . with good Strong Iron Hinges and a Substantial Lock fitting for Such a Doore Two Front Windows Two foot High and Eighteen Inches Wide with proper Iron Grates." Yet many jails continued to be in a state of disrepair, and some became distinctly foul places. Thomas Bell successfully protested his one-day sentence because "the heat of the Season and the Loathsomeness of the prison . . . , tends to the prejudice of his health." The court allowed him to sit out his sentence in "any place." As time passed, conditions in jails improved. According to Davis' handbook, prisoners each day were to be provided with a pound of bread and "dressed Meat" and two quarts of water. Yet even if jails were relatively comfortable and secure, the jailer himself might be negligent. James Bremen, responsible for watching the Edenton jail one night, simply "left the sayd Charge" at one or two in the morning. And John Cheely, jail keeper for Bath, was accused of unlawfully jailing a merchant and charging him 20s. for his release.[15]

In principle, judges had little discretion when it came to punishing serious offenders. Felons would be sentenced "expressly as by the Law directed for the Offence." All felonies with the exception of petit larceny, a crime penalized by whipping, required forfeiture of property or a sentence of death. The assembly reiterated this fact in 1764, when serious crimes were on the rise, by warning murderers, counterfeiters, and other felons that a "Judgment of Death may be passed against" them.[16]

14. General Court Minutes, October, 1698, NCHCR, III, 241; act of 1715, NCSR, XXIII, 22; May, 1732, Bertie County Court Minutes, 1724–43. For examples of charges against county officials, see March, 1734, March, 1735, General Court Sessions Docquet, 1734–36; and March, 1739, General Court Dockets, 1739.
15. Act of 1741, NCSR, XXIII, 181; December, 1736, Carteret County Court Minutes, 1723–47; Petition of Thomas Bell, General Court Minutes, 1732; Davis, Justice of Peace, 136; Crown v. Bremen, October, 1731, General Court Minutes, 1731–32; Crown v. Cheely, August, 1739, General Court Criminal Papers, 1738–39.
16. Davis, Justice of Peace, 216; Blackstone, Commentaries, IV, 94–98; act of 1764, NCSR, XXIII, 616.

Despite the general English prescription that capital offenders be punished at the gallows, North Carolina law did not always require execution. Harsh but non-capital penalties for animal stealing prevailed in the colony from a very early time, reflecting the value of livestock and the difficulty of protecting it. Beginning in 1715, killing, stealing, or mismarking horses, cattle, or hogs led to a fine of £10 above the value of the animal. Showing some sensitivity to a family's loss of male labor, the law provided different sanctions for married and single men. A married offender who could not pay the fine received "at the Whipping post or in the Court yard Twenty stripes on his bare back" for the first offense, thirty-nine for the second, and banishment thereafter. A single man, who might be penniless as well, escaped the lash, but could expect to spend two years in servitude. In 1741 the assembly imposed even harsher penalties to combat a rise in animal stealing. The sanction now included both a £10 fine and corporal punishment. First offenders could be whipped forty times and second offenders would "stand in the Pillory Two Hours, and be branded in the left Hand, with a red hot iron, with the letter T." By 1774, the English statute on horse stealing was also enforceable in the colony, making it a felony without benefit of clergy.[17]

Once again, despite prescribed sanctions in the statute law, judges used their discretion when sentencing cattle thieves. In 1738, for example, when the minimum fine was £10, the circuit court in Newton fined laborer Thomas Nixon 12s. 10d. for stealing and killing a steer, and William Horton, a calf thief, 5s. Two years later a Perquimans County court ordered James Thomas to pay £5 for stealing a heifer. And when two cattle thieves pleaded guilty in a Pasquotank County court the same year, their fine was still more lenient—£2 10s. If judges showed some sympathy for a man who, perhaps desperate for food, stole a steer, they had none at all for a horse thief. Between 1763 and 1772, every recorded sentence for horse theft was the penalty required by law—death without clergy. This was a crime of a basest kind, committed in no sense out of human need, but out of pure avarice.[18]

Counterfeiting was another capital crime for which the Carolina

17. Act of 1715, act of 1741, NCSR, XXIII, 58–59, 166; Davis, Justice of Peace, 205.
18. Crown v. George Nixon and Thomas Nixon and Crown v. Horton, January, 1738, General Court Criminal Papers, 1738–39; Crown v. Thomas, October, 1740, Perquimans County Court Minutes, 1738–42; Crown v. Cartwright and Crown v. Prichard, January, 1740, Pasquotank County Court Minutes, April, 1737–July, 1753; Herrup, "Law and Morality," 114–15.

courts imposed non-capital penalties. It was also a crime on the rise in the mid-eighteenth century, a fact that led the assembly to take special action. Recognizing this growing threat to a commercializing economy, legislators mandated in 1748 that first offenders be punished with up to forty lashes, two hours in the pillory, "and have both Ears nailed to the Pillory and cut off." Second offenders faced death without benefit of clergy. In 1764, all counterfeiters, by law, would be executed. Unfortunately, clerks rarely recorded sentences for convicted counterfeiters, but the penalties they did write down suggest that while punishment was harsh, death could be avoided. A higher court in 1764, for example, fined Joseph Hall £25, had him stand in the pillory for two hours, and, if the record is to be believed, gave him thirty-nine lashes. But mercifully Hall did not lose his ears. Two years later the same court allowed Jeremiah Barnet, a planter, to escape with twenty-nine lashes and one hour in the pillory only, though the death penalty was at that time required.[19]

The pattern of mitigation of penalties continues when punishment for theft is considered. Herein a complex amalgam of statute and common law tied the penalty to the value of the stolen goods and the way they were taken. If the stolen goods were valued at less than a shilling, and were not taken from a person or a house, the crime was petit larceny, punishable by whipping. If the stolen property was valued at more than a shilling, the crime was grand larceny, punishable by death, but clergyable for the first offense.[20] Mixed larceny, stealing from a person or a house, generally resulted in death without benefit of clergy. The crime of robbery (violently stealing from a person) or burglary (stealing by breaking into and entering a house at night) also led to death without clergy. As harsh as these penalties may seem, they could still be tempered, where allowable, by benefit of clergy and by downgrading the offense. In North Carolina, clergy was permitted "in all Cases where Clergy is not expressly taken away, or where the Offender has not once before had Clergy allow'd." On this point, judges never deviated from the law. Not a single criminal received clergy when the law

19. Act of 1748, act of 1764, NCSR, XXIII, 295, 616; Crown v. Hall, March, 1764, Salisbury District Court Trial and Minute Docket, 1761–90; Crown v. Barnet, March, 1766, Salisbury District Court Minutes, Superior Court, 1756–70.

20. Exceptions were horse theft and plundering shipwrecks, for example. Those were not clergyable offenses.

denied it. Another way of mitigating severe penalties—downgrading an offense—was a common practice used by English and American juries.[21] Blackstone noted with some displeasure that "The mercy of jurors often made them strain a point, and bring in larceny to be under the value of twelvepence, when it was really of much greater value." Yet this practice gave jurors an opportunity to consider a defendant's unique circumstances when they arrived at a verdict, thereby lessening the harshness of the law. When Thomas Gray, laborer, was indicted for stealing wool, nails, cotton, and linen, "all of the value of twenty Shillings," a capital offense, the jury convicted him of stealing ten pence worth of goods, thus making his crime petit larceny. Mary Cotton, a spinster, charged with taking some sixty shillings' worth of goods, was convicted of petit larceny of "Goods to the value of ten pence."[22]

Juries could also moderate sentences for convicted murderers. If the jurors determined that the killing was done without evil intent, then they could find the defendant guilty of manslaughter, clergyable for the first offense, or of chance medley, a pardonable act. In 1766 the Salisbury District Court indicted one Diedrick Neff for murder, but convicted him of chance medley, a killing in self-defense. The Wilmington District Court charged Lawrence Griffiths with murder, found him guilty of manslaughter, and ordered that he be burned on the hand. The message of these cases is clear. Despite the prescription that "In all capital Cases, the Court cannot alter or mitigate the Judgment," the courts had ways of doing so.[23]

In lessening the harshness of the formal law, colonial courts did no more than did their English counterparts.[24] But the colonies went even further, citing far fewer capital crimes in their criminal codes. Death in

21. Blackstone, *Commentaries,* IV, 229–47; Davis, *Justice of Peace,* 178. See Hawkins, *A Treatise of the Pleas of the Crown,* II, 440; Beattie, "Crime and the Courts in Surrey," in Cockburn (ed.), *Crime in England,* 172; Goebel and Naughton, *Law Enforcement in Colonial New York,* 675; Hull, "Female Felons," 70; and Hoffer and Scott (eds.), *Criminal Proceedings in Colonial Virginia,* liv.

22. Blackstone, *Commentaries,* IV, 239; *Crown v. Gray,* October, 1726, and *Crown v. Cotton,* March, 1724, NCHCR, VI, 323, 27–28.

23. *Crown v. Neff,* March, 1766, Salisbury District Court Minutes, Superior Court, 1756–70; *Crown v. Griffiths,* April, 1767, Wilmington District Court Minutes, Superior Court, 1760–83; Davis, *Justice of Peace,* 216.

24. Langbein, "Shaping the Eighteenth-Century Criminal Trial," 47. Also see Hay, "Property, Authority and the Criminal Law," in Hay *et al., Albion's Fatal Tree,* 18; Powers, *Crime and Punishment in Early Massachusetts,* 252; Chapin, *Criminal Justice in Colonial America,* 57.

North Carolina, for example, only awaited those convicted of certain crimes on the rise. Murderers and counterfeiters, according to legislation in 1764, would be executed. In his manual published ten years later, James Davis pointed to just six crimes (counterfeiting, homicide, robbery, arson, rape, and prison escape) for which the punishment was death. Even when the death penalty was required, few people were actually ordered to hang for their crimes. Only sixty-seven death sentences appear in the records—thirty for theft, twenty for homicide, thirteen for animal stealing, two for treason, and two for counterfeiting. And one-third of these sentences were remitted through benefit of clergy (twenty-one), pardon (two), and deportation (one). Many of the rest of the sentences may not have been carried out, for the evidence of actual executions is sparse. The tiny sample consists of an order for the execution of James Butler, horse thief, and a receipt for the expense of executing William Lisles for murder.[25]

In comparison to modern-day practices, the corporal punishment meted out by colonial courts may seem inhumane. Physical punishment did, in fact, constitute a sizable segment of all sentences, and when it came to whipping, a minimum of twenty-one lashes was the favored choice of the Carolina courts. At the same time, the barbarous penalties of legend do not often appear in the records. Until 1748, no required criminal sentence included maiming, and then only for one offense—counterfeiting. And when the courts ordered some kind of physical harm, an unusual situation might explain it. Sentences tended to be more severe in the seventeenth century when the council, for example, ordered Samuel Pricklove to "stand in the pillory three hours, and loose his right ear," or the General Court decreed that Stephen Manwaring, in addition to a year's confinement, "lose one of his Eares" for forgery. The only other similar recorded punishment was imposed by a county court on three black offenders, possibly slaves, in 1769. Moreover, while the records rarely show that physical punishments were actually carried out, occasionally the evidence says they were not. Bryan Conner, for example, convicted of petit larceny in 1741 and sentenced to an extreme penalty of sixty lashes, avoided the whipping because he "was in a very sick and low condition." Roger Snell, a convicted thief granted benefit of clergy, escaped the traditional branding on the thumb because "of his

25. Act of 1764, *NCSR*, XXIII, 616; Davis, *Justice of Peace*, 107, 174; Order for execution, April, 1736, General Court Criminal Papers, 1735–37; Report of the Committee of Public Claims, December 4, 1758, *NCSR*, V, 980.

very greivous sickness and weakness of Body." Thomas Dereham, whose crime was manslaughter, accomplished the same by getting a suspension of sentence until his case could be reviewed by the Crown.[26]

The most common punishment imposed by the Carolina courts was a monetary fine (Table 26).[27] Nearly three-quarters of all financial sanctions, most of which applied to misdemeanor offenses, amounted to less than a pound (Table 27). By imposing small penalties and allowing offenders to return quickly to their tasks in life, judges recognized that their crimes posed no great threat to society. As extensively as they were used in North Carolina, monetary fines offer a clue to the colony's general economic condition. If fines had a twofold purpose (to punish the offender and to defray government costs), and if there would be no reason to impose fines on those who could not pay, the frequency of these penalties indicates a small indigent class of criminals. Admittedly, where the law offered a choice of monetary or physical sanction, the penniless had no choice at all. But the records are curiously silent about cases in which indigent offenders had to face the pillory, the lash, or servitude. Joseph Castleton, for example, had pleaded guilty to contempt and sedition in 1724, but, "not having visible effects whereon to levy a fine," he then had to "stand in the pillory on the publick parade" for two hours. Mary Cotton, a spinster convicted of a petit larceny, faced sale "to Any person the highest bidder," if she could not pay a hefty amount for security and court costs. Besides these two cases, evidence from the records also shows that only four servants were penalized with an extended contract because they had no money.[28] Given so few cases of this kind, it seems offenders did, on the whole, pay their fines.

If there is an eighteenth-century punishment that challenges the more humane approach to criminal sanctions today, it was whipping. This was the physical sanction favored by the Carolina courts. In fact, neither disfigurement nor time in the pillory or stocks was a common penalty.

26. Council Minutes, March, 1680, *NCHCR*, II, 9; *Crown v. Manwaring*, July, 1698, *NCHCR*, III, 226; *Crown v. Negro Dick, Negro Jacob, and Negro Harry*, July, 1769, Johnston County Court Minutes, 1767–77; *Crown v. Conner*, 1741, *NCSR*, IV, 597; *Crown v. Snell*, March, 1698, *NCHCR*, III, 194–95; *Crown v. Dereham*, July, 1702, *NCHCR*, IV, 33–34.

27. For a similar pattern in other colonies, see Powers, *Crime and Punishment in Early Massachusetts*, 415–16; Chapin, *Criminal Justice in Colonial America*, 51, 53; Goebel and Naughton, *Law Enforcement in Colonial New York*, 705, 709; and Preyer, "Penal Measures in the American Colonies," 350.

28. See Preyer, "Penal Measures in the American Colonies," 350; *Crown v. Castleton* and *Crown v. Cotton*, March, 1724, *NCHCR*, VI, 26, 28.

TABLE 26
CRIMINAL SENTENCES, 1663–1776

Monetary		Whipping		Stocks/Pillory	Death	Other
770 (75.71%)		103 (10.12%)		17 (1.67%)	67 (6.58%)[a]	60 (5.89%)
Amount	Number	Amount	Number			
£ 1	558	10	12			
1–5	182	11–20	30			
6–10	20	21–40	50			
11–20	4	40	2			
21–30	3	unknown	9			
31–40	1					
41–50	1					
100	1					

NOTE: The table is based on 1,017 total penalties. Some of those sentenced received more than one kind of penalty.

"Other" column refers to banishment, carting, jail, loss of ear, etc.

[a]Includes 21 benefit of clergy, 2 pardons, and 1 deportation.

TABLE 27
SENTENCE, BY CRIME, 1663–1776

	Assault	Theft	Morals Crimes	Trespass	Animal Stealing	Contempt	Crimes Against Public Order	Homicide
Less than £1	308 (77.39%)	5 (4.81%)	38 (48.71%)	35 (76.09%)	3 (8.82%)	17 (45.95%)	13 (61.90%)	—
£1–£5	83 (20.85)	4 (3.85)	16 (20.51)	10 (21.74)	7 (20.58)	9 (24.32)	5 (23.80)	—
£6–£10	3 (0.75)	—	4 (5.12)	1 (2.17)	—	4 (10.81)	1 (4.76)	—
1–20 lashes	—	23 (22.11)	7 (8.97)	—	3 (8.82)	—	—	—
21–39 lashes	2 (0.50)	30 (28.84)	1 (1.28)	—	3 (8.82)	—	—	—
40 or more lashes	—	2 (1.92)	—	—	—	—	—	—
Death	—	30 (28.84)a	—	—	13 (38.23)	—	—	20 (86.95%)b
Other	2 (0.50)	10 (9.61)	12 (15.38)	—	5 (14.70)	7 (18.91)	2 (9.52)	3 (13.04)
Total	398 (99.99)	104 (99.98)	78 (99.97)	46 (100)	34 (99.97)	37 (99.99)	21 (99.98)	23 (99.99)

aIncludes 13 benefit of clergy and 1 deportation.
bIncludes 8 benefit of clergy.

Corporal punishment was usually the lot of two kinds of criminals—the most egregious morals offenders and thieves. Evidence on these particular offenses makes it possible, in a small way, to see in sharper focus how judges and juries reacted to individual cases. Christian Finney, for example, convicted of the most odious form of bastardy—bearing a mulatto child—received a harsh sentence of fifteen lashes. John Hassell's penalty of thirty-nine lashes "for Speaking Prophane and Irreverent words" on the Sabbath was exceedingly severe. But Hassell had already made frequent court appearances for irreverent behavior and adultery. Thieves could expect a firm response from the court if they were repeat offenders or if they showed no contrition. James Fant, laborer, was convicted of two different thefts in 1742. He first stole a coat valued at one shilling, and then an assortment of items including pork, a pewter dish, a meal sifter, and a large sword. For the second offense, he was sentenced to death. Here the higher court bench reacted firmly to a second-time thief who stole goods not for survival but for avarice. In 1727 the General Court convicted laborer William Hughes of two thefts, which, by law, should have resulted in his execution. Instead, he received thirty-nine lashes plus a branding on "the hand with the Letter: T." Having confessed to both indictments and asked for mercy, Hughes established himself as no hardened criminal but as a man full of remorse.[29]

A court's personal response to individual cases is seen most clearly when judges resorted to a particular form of punishment—carting, or wearing labels. This was not a common sanction, for only ten appear in the records. Nor were these penalties often employed elsewhere in America.[30] But this form of punishment could be closely tailored to the crime and the offender. Usually the crime was minor. After Mary Silva was convicted of blasphemy in 1765, she was to be "Carted about town with labells on her back & breast espressing her crime, for one hour, and afterwards stand in the Pillory for one hour more." Andrew Campbell, a perjurer, faced a carting "up and down the Town from One end to the

29. *Crown* v. *Finney,* June, 1741, Carteret County Court Dockets, 1731–62; *Crown* v. *Hassell,* March, 1722, NCHCR, V, 289 (earlier court appearances: *Crown* v. *Hassell,* March, November, 1720, March, 1721, NCHCR, V, 214, 225–26, 241); *Crown* v. *Fant,* May, 1742, General Court Criminal Papers, 1740–44, and General Court Minute Dockets—Miscellaneous Dockets, 1680–1754; *Crown* v. *Hughes,* October, 1727, NCHCR, VI, 456–57.

30. Goebel and Naughton, *Law Enforcement in Colonial New York,* 706–707; Powers, *Crime and Punishment in Early Massachusetts,* 198–201; Preyer, "Penal Measures in the American Colonies," 335.

other with a Rope about his Neck and with the Word PURJURY wrote in Cappetol Letters on his Forehead and that he stop at every House and then to Stand Hour in the pillory." Kate, a free Negro convicted of "poison," was "whipped at carts-tail on 3 distinct succeeding Wednesdays."[31] Each of these sanctions involved pain and humiliation, a combination of penalties that the courts hoped would keep the offender and all those who observed his or her punishment from appearing in court again.

To what extent did variables such as status, gender, and race influence a particular sentence? Studies suggest that class did play a role in sentencing practices. From the records of early New Haven and Massachusetts, offenders who were of higher status were typically fined while men and women of lower status were whipped.[32] Indeed, the Carolina courts were more likely to fine men of means than those less well off and were less likely to sentence them to the lash.[33] This finding is predictable, since some degree of class discrimination was already built into the criminal code. Legislation of 1715, for example, provided for a whipping or sale into servitude, depending on marital status, for animal thieves who could not pay the fine. The law called for a maximum of twenty-one lashes for impoverished fornicators. A similar law in 1741 created a separate standard of justice for servants who presumably had no financial means: "whereby Persons free are punishable by Fine, Servants shall be punished by whipping . . . unless the Servant so culpable can and will procure some Person or Persons to pay the Fine." Despite such laws, which from all indications put the poor at a disadvantage, the Carolina records show that this did not in fact necessarily happen. Conventional methodology, in a consideration of status and punishment, fails to relate sentences to actual crimes and so disregards the possibility that men of higher status committed a larger proportion of finable offenses. Indeed, when the Carolina data are broken down, the

31. *Crown v. Silva,* March, 1765, Salisbury District Court Trial and Minute Docket, 1761–90; *Crown v. Campbell,* March, 1768, Salisbury District Court Crown Docket, Superior Court, 1767–79; *Crown v. Kate,* May, 1763, New Bern District Court Trial, Argument, Reference, and Appearance Docket, 1758–60.

32. See M. P. Baumgartner, "Law and Social Status in Colonial New Haven, 1639–1665," *Research in Law and Sociology,* I (1978), 168–70; Faber, "Puritan Criminals," 135; Chapin, *Criminal Justice in Colonial America,* 53.

33. Fifty-eight planters (90.62 percent), among those whose sentences are known, received a monetary fine; fifteen laborers (68.18 percent), among those whose sentences are known, received a monetary fine. Six planters (9.37 percent) and seven laborers (31.81 percent) were given corporal punishment.

result suggests no class bias at all. For each of five common offenses (assault, theft, homicide, animal stealing, and trespass), the courts sentenced planters and laborers to an identical proportion of corporal and monetary sanctions. While the records offer no explicit evidence that any particular bench showed sympathy for a poor defendant, John Dickson's case, rare as it is, suggests that some courts did. After the Wilmington District Court acquitted Dickson of an unnamed offense, officers of the court, including the chief justice, Crown attorney, sheriff, and clerk, all "forgave him their fees it having appeared that he was a poor man & not able to pay the same."[34] One case does not prove a point, but together with the other evidence offered here, the Carolina data convey the strong impression that sentencing practices were largely status blind.

Nor do the data show that Carolina women, like their counterparts in other colonies, were punished more severely or more leniently than were men.[35] Overall, women were sent to the whipping post at a much higher rate than were men and fined at a much lower rate.[36] Once again, when the data are broken down, when individual offenses are considered (assault and theft), men and women received corporal and financial sanctions at nearly the same rate (Table 28). Only for adultery and fornication, common female crimes, are real differences in male and female sentences apparent. Does this suggest harsher treatment for women who violated the moral code? The answer is both yes and no. A larger proportion of physical punishments for women may reflect the fact that women, as a group, lacked the financial means of men. Females convicted of adultery or fornication and unable to pay the fine might have to undergo a whipping instead. Winifrid Morris, who confessed to "haveing a Basterd Child," faced this kind of choice in 1707 when the General Court ordered her to "be punished by receiving Twenty one Stripes on her bare Back or pay fifty Shillings with Costs." Yet the evidence, sparse though it is, points to a minimal impact of gender on punishment for morals crimes. In 1697, for example, the General Court

34. Act of 1715, act of 1741, *NCSR,* XXIII, 5, 58–59, 194; *Crown* v. *Dickson,* October, 1763, Wilmington District Court Minutes, Superior Court, 1760–83.

35. See Hull, "Female Felons," 151–52; Freedman, "Their Sisters' Keepers," 8–9; Semmes, *Crime and Punishment in Early Maryland,* 180.

36. Seven hundred seven men (91.93 percent), among those whose sentences are known, received monetary fines; eighty-one women (77.88 percent), among those whose sentences are known, received a monetary fine. Sixty-two (8.06 percent) men and twenty-three women (22.11 percent) were given corporal punishment.

TABLE 28
SENTENCE BY CRIME, BY SEX, 1663–1776

	Assault		Theft		Adultery/Fornication	
	M	F	M	F	M	F
Monetary fine	372 (99.47%)	23 (100.00%)	8 (13.79%)	2 (15.38%)	24 (96.00%)	16 (84.21%)
Corporal punishment	2 (0.53)	—	50 (86.21)	11 (84.62)	1 (4.00)	3 (15.79)

ordered that adulterers Thomas Stanton and Mary Jones "Be punished by receiving Each of them twenty stripes." In later years, county courts imposed the same penalties on partners in immorality. The Edgecombe County bench fined Richard Thomas and Rebecca Lewis one shilling each; a Halifax County court required that two couples each pay one penny.[37]

White law distinguished itself vividly and prejudicially from black law in statutory provisions for punishing slave crime. If slavery was to survive, particularly after mid-century, when the black population was so rapidly on the rise, then absolute discipline had to be maintained.[38] One form was the exceedingly harsh and sometimes grisly and public punishment for slaves who committed crimes. Carolina lawmen proceeded piecemeal, beginning in 1715, to work out a means by which punishment could effectively sustain submission at a minimal loss to slaveowners. Despite the fact that white criminals were pilloried, lashed, and sometimes maimed, and that physical sanctions were apparently accepted as the norm, slave punishment was still indisputably more severe.

When freeholders courts were created in 1715 to try slaves accused of crimes, punishment was left to the "best Judgment & Discretion" of the bench. Here justices were not limited by traditional English law. Sanctions could affect "life or Member" or include "any other Corporal Punishment." No loss to the slaveowner would result, for if a slave was executed or killed while fleeing, the court established his or her value so that the owner could be compensated from a public account. In 1741 the assembly reacted both to the fear of insurrection created by the recent Stono Rebellion and to a growing problem in slave societies—slave runaways. Now slaves (and servants as well) who ran away could be whipped as many as thirty-nine times, "as the said Justice shall think fit." If they were caught with an illegal weapon, a gun, sword, or club, the penalty was twenty-one lashes. For the first time in the colony's history, a slave could be outlawed. This provision applied directly to the large number of men and women who concealed themselves for long

37. *Crown v. Morris,* March, 1707, NCHCR, IV, 334; *Crown v. Stanton and Jones,* October, 1697, NCHCR, III, 89; *Crown v. Thomas and Lewis,* November, 1755, Edgecombe County Court Crown Docket, 1755–56; *Crown v. Jarrell and Hill,* May, 1769, *Crown v. Crowley and Jones,* August, 1769, Halifax County Court Crown Docket, 1759–70.

38. See Winthrop Jordan, *White Over Black: American Attitudes Toward the Negro, 1550–1812* (Chapel Hill, 1968), 103–35.

periods of time "in the Swamps, Woods and other Obscure Places." An outlawed slave who refused to surrender himself became, in effect, the prey of white predators who could "kill and destroy [him] by such Ways and Means as he or she shall think fit." Without equivocating, the law of 1741 also prescribed a single penalty for conspiracy—death. Twelve years later, the assembly altered slightly the law on slave executions—a perverse hint that white law was not cold-blooded through and through. Now the owners of slaves killed as outlaws or executed for crimes would not receive compensation unless they could demonstrate that the slave had been adequately clothed and fed.[39] Yet it should also be said that the assembly hoped to reduce the number of compensations. Certainly that helped motivate the law of 1758, which warned owners that they would not recover the value of slaves executed for crimes committed while hired out or of slaves brought from "foreign parts" who had already committed crimes. The assembly also moved in that year to join other colonies in providing for a gory and repugnant punishment that had no model in English law—castration. Between 1759 and 1764, when the law was repealed, "no male Slave shall for the First Offence, be condemned to Death, unless for Murder or Rape." Instead, he would be castrated. While this punishment would spare the colony the expense of an executed slave, it was also fraught with meaning about the proper place of white women and about black male sexuality. Its removal in 1764 perhaps signified a humanitarian effort or a desire to put unruly slaves to death rather than to discipline them after castration.[40]

Recorded punishments actually meted out to the slaves by the freeholders courts range from castration to hanging and from burning to branding on the cheek. Clearly, however harsh white penalties may have been, penalties for blacks were worse. Consider four indictments of Negroes Duke, Jacob, Harry, and Coffee in Johnston County in 1769. Convicted of an unnamed offense, they all received forty lashes and had both ears cut off. When white lawmen tried to petrify potentially errant slaves, they punished offenders in a truly grisly way. In 1770, for example, a Duplin County court, having convicted George of rape, ordered

39. Act of 1715, NCSR, XXIII, 64; Marvin L. Michael Kay and Lorin Lee Cary, " 'The Planters Suffer Little or Nothing': North Carolina Compensations for Executed Slaves, 1748–1772," Science and Society, XL (1976), 288–306; act of 1741, NCSR, XXIII, 199–204; Kay and Cary, "Slave Runaways in Colonial North Carolina," 4–5; act of 1753, NCSR, XXIII, 390.

40. Act of 1758, NCSR, XXIII, 488–89; Jordan, White Over Black, 154–58; act of 1764, NCSR, XXIII, 656. Also see Kay and Cary, " 'The Planters Suffer Little or Nothing,' " 299.

TABLE 29
SENTENCE BY CRIME, BY COURT, 1663–1776

Court	Assault				Theft			
	Monetary Fine		Corporal Punishment		Monetary Fine		Corporal Punishment	
General	30	(96.77%)	1	(3.23%)	4	(16.00%)	21	(84.00%)
Superior	94	(100.00)	—	—	4	(16.00)	21	(84.00)
County	255	(99.61)	1	(0.39)	2	(11.76)	15	(88.24)

that he "hang by the Neck untill he be dead, and then his head to be Severed from his Body and Stuck up at the Forks of the Road." Another convicted rapist, Ben, was to "be Hanged by the Neck untill he be Dead that his Head be Severed from his Body . . . put upon a pole . . . and afterwards his Body be Burn't." No instance of such maiming of whites, alive or dead, appears in the eighteenth-century records. Nor did many whites receive thirty-nine lashes for assault, as did Rob, a slave, for attacking Thomas Winter in 1738.[41] Comparisons of death penalties for whites and slaves show a lopsided number of black executions. Between 1663 and 1776, approximately forty-two free men and women were sentenced to death without clergy; at least one hundred slave criminals were executed between 1748 and 1772.[42]

Even the formal law unreservedly assigned different punishments to whites and blacks for the same crime—animal stealing. In 1741 a slave convicted of the first offense would "suffer both his Ears to be Cut off, and be publickly whipt." For the second offense, the penalty was death. Cato was a first offender convicted of hog stealing in 1748. A Craven County court ordered the sheriff to "take the said Negro Cato to the Publick whiping Post & there to Nail his Ears to the said Post & them Cut off." Forty lashes constituted the second part of his penalty. Sanctions for white offenders, albeit harsh by modern standards, were limited to fines, whipping, the pillory, or branding on the thumb.[43] In every

41. Kay and Cary, "'The Planters Suffer Little or Nothing,'" 292; July, 1769, Johnston County Court Minutes, 1767–77; Crown v. George, May, 1770, Secretary of State, Court Records, Magistrates and Freeholders Courts; Crown v. Ben, September, 1775, Treasurer and Comptroller, Miscellaneous Group, 1738–1909; Crown v. Rob, March, 1739, General Court Criminal Papers, 1738–39.

42. See Kay and Cary, "'They are Indeed the Constant Plague,'" 49.

43. Act of 1741, NCSR, XXIII, 167; Crown v. Cato, February, 1748, Miscellaneous Collections, Slavery Papers, 1747–1850.

TABLE 30
SENTENCE BY DECADE

	1720s	1730s	1740s	1750s	1760s	1770s
Monetary fine	12 (44.44%)	40 (97.56%)	62 (95.38%)	117 (95.12%)	341 (89.03%)	178 (94.18%)
Corporal punishment	15 (55.56)	1 (2.44)	3 (4.62)	6 (4.88)	42 (10.97)	11 (5.82)

way possible, then, the law made an enslaved black less than a person. And if a slave broke the law, punishment could be both arbitrary and brutal. This in itself served two purposes. First, humiliating and crippling penalties inflicted on blacks helped to lay to rest questions about the rationale of slavery. And second, in a paradoxical way, the savage punishments inflicted on slaves made more humane white sanctions possible.

When considering the crimes of slaves and free men and women, judges and juries, like their English counterparts, adopted punishments to fit their own needs. They arrived at penalties that reflected social norms, however debased, for servants and slaves; the formal law; and their own perception of the criminal and the crime. For two offenses—assault and theft—judges were remarkably consistent in sentencing (Table 29). Men sitting on the bench of the county or higher courts almost always penalized an assault with a fine. The offense required neither public humiliation nor physical pain. Some form of corporal punishment, however, awaited convicted thieves. Wherever their cases were tried, they could expect a painful sanction. Whether it was the pillory, the stocks, or the lash, thieves put private property in jeopardy and were punished accordingly.

By modern standards, white punishment was harsh, black punishment was diabolic. Little in the records points to an amelioration of penalties for blacks, but there is every indication that with the passage of time, the regular courts gradually imposed a declining proportion of corporal punishments.[44] Only during the 1720s, a particularly chaotic period that preceded the dramatic expansion of the colony and the courts, was the proportion of physical and financial sanctions nearly the same (Table 30). Exceedingly harsh punishment was not the rule for whites, nor was a different standard of punishment based on class or gender. The surviving data do not support the conclusion that men of means received more moderate criminal sanctions than did those who had little or nothing. Nor does the evidence point to leniency for women.

44. Hoffer found that penalties in Virginia got more severe. See Hoffer and Scott (eds.), *Criminal Proceedings in Colonial Virginia,* lxxii.

VII

LAW ENFORCEMENT IN THE CAROLINA WORLD

On an October day in 1686, somewhere in the Carolina woods, a fledgling colonial government held a higher court at the house of William Foster. What took place differed substantially from proprietary plans. Yet these early settlers were merely working out a problem that faced all colonial governments—how to build a law enforcement structure in the wilderness. The Carolina proprietors offered little guidance. Their complicated system of courts and personnel would fail, even in the best of circumstances. Perhaps without intending to, the proprietors left the colony largely on its own to secure law and order thousands of miles from home. As much as they could, given their isolation, the early settlers followed the fundamental principles of English law and procedure. At Foster's house, council members presided over a court that handled fifteen different pieces of business, including two indictments and a jury trial.[1] Gradually the Carolina courts moved on to more permanent sites, and law enforcement practices more closely approximated English ways. But it was North Carolina's own history of slow growth, political strife, and slow economic progress that ultimately determined what its legal institutions and practices would be.

Perhaps the most jarring chapter in the history of Carolina law enforcement is the recurrent internal strife that often threw the colony into turmoil. New leadership, factionalism, and imperial disputes created, at times, a swirl of political chaos. Yet these troubles produced no permanent institutional decay. True, on occasion the courts closed down and

1. *NCHCR*, II, 371–73.

criminals no doubt escaped prosecution. But in the larger view, the activity of the Carolina courts is far more impressive than are their periods of inertia. Nothing tells this story more clearly than the thousands of loose papers and carefully bound documents that depict eighteenth-century criminal justice at work. Indeed, criminal justice had to work, for in a society of English men and women, however remote, the law of necessity helped to hold the delicate strands of the social structure together. Weakened as they were by the push and pull of politics and personalities, Carolina legal institutions could still provide a stable underpinning for a fragile social base. In the absence of the social hierarchy of an older world, the daily operation of law enforcement brought North Carolina's own fuzzy social distinctions into sharper focus. Here the men of property, with their unremarkable holdings, could set the areas of control not just for themselves but also for those who had little or nothing. Yet the law was always much more than malleable clay in the hands of elites. Outside the formal environment of the courts, every colonist, the poorest and the meanest among them, could help define limits of control by their inclusion in apprehending and securing suspects. And in a less visible way, all the values and legal decisions from North Carolina's English past were intrinsic to the colony's own legal system. These elements could not be tampered with.[2] From this perspective, the history of early Carolina is, so to speak, turned upside down. Seen through the lens of law enforcement, a legal system so long noted for its frailty actually served as a linchpin of stability.

Carolina law enforcers had all the strengths and weaknesses of their counterparts in other colonies. Typically, there was nothing special in their background to prepare them for their tasks. Their legal training was often as sparse as their experience. But their lack of preparation need not have hampered their ability to administer criminal justice. In the first place, the colonial frontier did not require sophisticated practices, and law enforcement there probably functioned better without them. Second, North Carolina law enforcers had access to laymen's legal manuals that defined their responsibilities and provided a rudimentary legal education. Besides these practitioner's guides, English legal works were available in the colony, at least in the private libraries of some justices and lawyers, and by mid-century, every court required a few

2. See Thompson's discussion of the influence of culture and the past on the law, in E. P. Thompson, *Whigs and Hunters: The Origin of the Black Act* (New York, 1975), 258–69.

standard treatises. Holding several offices could make lawmen more proficient. Whether the positions were simultaneous or individuals moved from one to another, usually taking an upward step, the experience was invaluable. Further, certain family names dominate lists of those in office, suggesting an incipient governing elite. These were not men of great wealth by the standards of other colonies, but they figured importantly in the Carolina world. Indeed, in a colony where great wealth was rare, government posts were an alternate means to advancement.

Almost from the beginning, Carolina rulers contended for power, fomenting political strife and disarray. Since they were lawmen as well, their own contentiousness not only created disorder but also made it difficult to control. The severe disruptions of the 1720s and the factionalism of the 1740s and 1750s stretched legal institutions nearly to the breaking point. Yet the system survived: it had to. Given the fragile underpinnings of North Carolina, a certain respect and regard for the law, however subtle, was a necessity. And respect for the law came not just from the top. Law enforcement rested heavily on community involvement and consent. Working in tandem with appointed lawmen, ordinary citizens also played a critical role. Victims had to come forward, witnesses had to give depositions or appear in court, friends or relatives of the accused had to ensure a court appearance, and men had to serve on juries. Each responsibility entailed no small sacrifice—personal risk, long distances to travel, little compensation—and usually no great reward. Yet the ordinary people of "poor" Carolina, "disgusting" in their equality and "wretchedly ignorant," still helped to make the wheels of justice turn. Despite internal conflict, slow growth, and the uncertain potential of vast, unsettled lands, North Carolina built at a notably early time a relatively sturdy legal structure that, for much of the time, held fast. Not surprisingly, a rural environment demanded it. Rural Carolina required a certain adherence to the formal rule of law, for simple necessity meant avoiding what the alternative might be.

Carolina society, from oppressed blacks to aspiring white elites, provided the cultural context for criminal justice practices. Given the constant presence of slaves, lawmen had to develop a separate scheme of law enforcement that would be appropriate to them. The task was not difficult. Virginia and West Indian colonies had already built control of slave crime into the statute law. But as the number of Negroes in North Carolina increased, white anxieties grew as well, leading to more specific and brutal legislation in 1741 and 1758. All laws that dealt with slave crimes reflected certain assumptions about the activities of blacks that did not apply to free whites. The ironic belief was that blacks, so separate from whites in so many ways, could still be guilty of crimes. The condition of bondage had no relevance to a theft or a murder. But there the sameness ended. For all practical purposes, slaves accused of crimes had no legal safeguards, short of a defense by themselves or their masters. Presumptions of innocence did not apply; nor did a jury's judgment of fact. English judges had some discretion, but the bench of the freeholders court had infinitely more. Slave punishment went far beyond humiliation and deterrence. It had to be vicious enough to terrify other slaves and, as a final solution, to remove the most stubborn and dangerous blacks from the world forever. Admittedly, white law could be vicious as well. But while a significant and steadily widening gap existed between white law and actual practice, no such trend toward humaneness benefited blacks. This suggests a perverse seesaw relationship between criminal justice for free whites and for slaves. As punishment became more cruel for slaves, it became more compassionate for whites.

The much larger sample of the records of the regular courts enhances certain nuances in North Carolina. Predictably, a large proportion of poor men came to court for property crimes. Men in better circumstances faced most often charges of violence against each other and against the government, and charges of immoral behavior. Apparently, poor whites knew their place. More prosecutions for antigovernment behavior—contempt, sedition, perjury—were made against men of means. Women also knew their place. Rarely accused of public crimes, they appeared in court for moral misbehavior and theft, two breaches of the law they could accomplish without emerging from their female constraints.

In a freeholders court, few variables influenced the findings of the bench. Little more than the stark reality of the situation, the fact that evidence pointed to a slave having committed a serious crime, impressed the judges. An entirely different scenario operated in the regular courts. Subtle as its impact was, status did matter. With men of property serving as judges and jurors, men of little or no means suffered. In the matter of crimes against property, to put it simply, poor men could expect a harsher legal judgment. Gender also perceptibly influenced decision making. Judged exclusively by men, women received overall harsher treatment than did male defendants. Courts were attentive, in particular, to their marital status. Married women who engaged in adultery were treated more leniently than were men, but single women accused of fornication were not.

Swayed by race, gender, and status, judicial decisions could also be affected by the crime itself. Here the disposition of particular cases serves as a mirror of the Carolina world. Contempt, assault, homicide, and moral misbehavior—crimes that put the social order in jeopardy— all tended toward high conviction rates. This fact alone portrays a society deeply concerned with preserving order—as North Carolina may well have been. Recurrent internal strife, especially in the early period, at mid-century, and during the Regulation, not only threatened social peace but also hindered economic growth. Offenses that led to low conviction rates—theft, trespass, and animal stealing—were against property and, admittedly, may have been difficult to prosecute. But given North Carolina's modest wealth and periodic violence, crimes against stability posed a greater threat to social cohesion than did crimes against property. Yet this was not always the case. Patterns of conviction changed with the times, reflecting the social environment. Consider, for example, the concurrent growth of the colony and the increase in theft convictions. As the economy generated more that was worth stealing, property crimes took on much greater importance for lawmen.

Because criminal court cases vary according to the fluctuation of crime in the society at large, they reflect community perceptions of crime and attitudes toward controlling it. The notably low rate of antigovernment offenses and correspondingly high rate of assault prosecutions are evidence that disorder in the colony was substantially personal rather than political. Not surprisingly, theft was the second most frequently prosecuted offense. Stealing could be a temporary antidote to poverty or could be motivated by greed. Even in a sparsely settled colony of limited material wealth, theft was still a vexing problem. Yet the proportion of theft charges relative to all others declined over time. This might indicate the growing effectiveness of deterrents or the expansion of the propertied class. The steady, persistent decline in morals charges is easily explained. As the colony matured, its religious foundation, never strong to begin with, weakened. With time, orthodoxy gave way to more secular concerns.

What do the criminal court records reveal about the practical effectiveness of criminal justice? The answer hinges, of course, on what the evidence from the records is measured against, and comparative data are rare. Keeping this in mind, and acknowledging as well the records' fallibility, we should review only the most objective and quantifiable evidence. What percentage of criminal charges did the courts dispose of, and how many cases did they fail to resolve? Was contempt a frequently prosecuted offense? Did government officials—justices of the peace, sheriffs, constables—figure importantly among the accused? Did complete juries convene? Did witnesses, suspects, and prosecutors appear in court as required? To what extent did the tools of law enforcement work well? Did jails hold their charges? And did the convicted return to court again, charged with other crimes?

The sum total of indicted charges (3,655) resulted in a conviction rate of 31.8 percent. In New York, which enjoyed a more mature system of law enforcement, the overall conviction rate reached 47.9 percent. However, the two colonies had similar records on unresolved cases—37 percent for New York and 39.7 percent for North Carolina. Moreover, beginning in 1730 and recurring in each successive decade, the proportion of unresolved Carolina cases declined. This notable trend failed to occur in the northern province.[3] Here the message is clear. With the passage of time and the corresponding evolution of legal institutions, lawmen became more proficient at handling a steadily growing volume of cases.

Did Carolina lawmen have to contend on a routine basis with colonists who challenged their authority? Contempt ranked high among a wide variety of crimes, reflecting a real weakness in law enforcement, one that plagued other colonies as well.[4] But the pattern of contempt charges across the whole span of the colonial period shows that this was no festering problem. Rather, a large proportion of all contempt charges occurred at a predictable time—the turbulent decades of the 1720s and 1730s. Thereafter, colonists seldom came to court for resisting authority. As fragile as it seemed at times, the government showed a growing ability to command popular respect.

Perhaps the most commonplace image of North Carolina is that of a colony torn and weakened by political rivalries and by self-interested and corrupt government officials. Yet the records are curiously silent

3. Greenberg, *Crime and Law Enforcement in New York,* 71, 206.
4. The rate of contempt charges in New York, for example, was 5.9 percent. See Greenberg, *Crime and Law Enforcement in New York,* 50.

about these predatory office-holders. All the data combined reveal only fourteen cases of negligence and twenty-one cases of extortion. Four convictions resulted. Perhaps unfit lawmen were not being brought to justice, and given that lawmen represented justice, this is a real possibility. But consider also that despite a handful of oft-quoted derisive comments about North Carolina justices, especially backcountry men, evidence from the courts suggests that law enforcers in general were neither especially corrupt nor incompetent.

If there was an unmistakably weak link in Carolina justice, it was the failure of jurors, witnesses, and defendants to answer their summons to court. Legislation time and again established fines for negligent jurymen, denoting how persistent this particular problem could be and how no attempt at reform could solve it. "Witness never came" and "defendant never came" are reasons given for only thirty-one case dismissals. But clerks rarely explained dismissals, and the actual number is no doubt substantially larger. It is difficult to examine the court records and not be impressed by the glaring number of unresolved cases. Community attitudes about crime are reflected in this phenomenon, perceptions about which kinds of misbehavior should be taken seriously. Also implicit but difficult to gauge is a certain amount of popular resistance to legal institutions that were, after all, created and managed by colonial elites.

One of the nuts and bolts of law enforcement—jails—also fell short of serving their intended purpose. While there are many complaints in the records about inadequate jails, the actual number of recorded jail escapes is relatively small—thirty-seven, or less than 1 percent of all prosecutions. Twenty-one cases for which an outcome is known resulted in only seven convictions, and clerks noted "defendant escaped" only three times during the entire colonial period. But these figures leave a false impression that jails were secure. Most suspects were in fact never detained in them, but were bound to appear at the next court session, and few of the convicted ever received a jail sentence. Foul conditions, crumbling walls, negligent jail-keepers, all discouraged courts from punishing by confinement. Time and again the local courts charged their counties with "keeping a bad prison." Ironically, this was a very modern-sounding problem. Eighteenth-century Carolina citizens, responsible through their county governments for maintaining jails, blazed a path for posterity by choosing to channel public resources elsewhere.

Perhaps the best test of colonial law enforcement was its ability to discourage criminal repeaters. At least 666 of 3,773 men and women charged with crimes were prosecuted more than once—a rate of 17.6 percent. The rate of recidivism in New York, for which comparative data are available, was strikingly similar—16.4 percent.[5] When roughly one in six suspects is someone who has been in court before, adequate deterrents to crime do not exist. Despite considerably harsher penalties for men and women convicted of successive crimes, they boldly committed them. An unknown number escaped prosecution altogether or went elsewhere to engage in crime. Habitual offenders constituted a real defect in eighteenth-century criminal justice, albeit one that modern-day systems have yet to correct.

If courts are a mirror of the world they govern, then eighteenth-century North Carolina, "poor" and "ignorant" as it may have been, achieved a significant level of sophistication. True, years went by in which fewer than ten criminal charges appear in the records, in which colonists complained that criminals evaded prosecution. But by mid-century, the courts handled a much larger number of cases and brought more to a resolution. Indeed, the role of criminal justice in the Carolina world went far beyond apprehending and convicting criminals. On a day-to-day basis, legal institutions were vital: they represented stability and imposed it. Law enforcement worked in part through the formal rules and procedures that created it. There was also a certain amount of inner discipline, built on beliefs and attitudes that regarded the law as a crucial component of the social order. For lawmen, criminal justice helped to preserve distinctions between elites and those below. But within a free white society, the law could also diminish the potential for conflict that such distinctions might create. Judges, for example, had a great deal of discretion to soften the edges of a harsh written law, and they used it. Courts could convict and punish, and they could also show mercy. Subject to heavy fines, morals offenders rarely had to pay them. Judges granted benefit of clergy, juries downgraded an offense. Herein the legal system, operated by men of property, could act benevolently toward lower-crust whites. Indeed, when it came to sentencing, status or gender simply did not matter much.

All the flaws in law enforcement no doubt took their toll—untrained

5. Greenberg, *Crime and Law Enforcement in New York,* 210.

lawmen; biases of gender, status, and race; negligent witnesses, jurors, and defendants; decrepit jails. Yet in the end, before the Revolution, North Carolina was a colony well acquainted with the law and as prepared as were any of the other colonies to deal with those who challenged it. In fact, students of early Carolina might do well to shift their focus from the inadequacy of lawmen to their increasing effectiveness, from the crudeness of Carolina life to its growing sophistication, and from politics and personalities as a source of disorder to law enforcement as a source of stability. To be sure, the maturation of the colony and the improving record of law enforcement were not much consolation to slaves. They experienced racial bias in an infinitely more savage form than poor whites experienced biases of gender and class. They did indeed live in a separate world, whether they committed crimes or not. The elites who wielded power, forever white and male, established their own needs and shielded them. In an increasingly effective way, criminal justice protected property against threats from the propertyless, secured women in their place, and, through cold manipulation of the English law, ensured the survival of slavery.

BIBLIOGRAPHY

PRIMARY SOURCES

COURT RECORDS

North Carolina State Department of Archives and History, Raleigh

GENERAL COURT

Minute Dockets—Miscellaneous Dockets, 1680–1754
Minute Docket, 1704–32
Papers, 1717–54
Criminal Papers, 1720–29
Minutes, 1725, 1727, 1730, 1731–32, 1732, 1733, 1736
Criminal Papers, 1730–34
Dockets, 1732, 1736, 1737, 1739, 1744
Sessions Docquet, 1734–36
Criminal Papers, 1735–37, 1738–39
Criminal Action Papers, 1735–46
Dockets, 1737, 1745–46
Docquet, July–October, 1739
Court of Assizes, 1739–42
Papers, 1740
Criminal Papers, 1740–44
Dockets, 1741
Docket, March–July–October, 1741
Reference Docket, July, 1741–October, 1742, partial
Docket, March–July–October, 1742

Docket, March–July–October, 1743
Docket, March–July, 1744
Dockets, 1745–46
Criminal Papers—General and Assize Courts, 1745–49
Dockets, 1746–47
Dockets, 1748–52
Criminal Papers—General, Assize, and Supreme Courts, 1750–59
Minutes, 1750–67
Dockets, 1752–53

SUPREME COURT

Minute Docket, October, 1755, October, 1756
Minute Docket, April, 1757–April, 1759

DISTRICT COURTS

Edenton
  Criminal Action Papers, 1756–1806
  Superior Court, Miscellaneous, n.d., 1760
  Minute Docket, November, 1760–67
  Records, 1761
  Records, 1763–64
  Records, 1764
  Records, 1765
  Crown Docket Superior Court, May, 1765–October, 1769
  Records, 1768
  Records, 1771
  Minutes, 1771–72
  Records, 1772–73
Halifax
  Miscellaneous Records, 1763–1808
Hillsborough
  Minute Dockets, 1768–83
New Bern
  Reference Docket, 1755–59
  Miscellaneous Records, 1758–1806
  Trial, Argument, Reference, and Appearance Docket, 1758–60,
    1769–70
  Criminal Action Papers, 1761–75
  Minutes, 1768–72, 1778–88

Salisbury
  Criminal Action Papers, 1754, 1756–59, 1760–71
  Minutes, Superior Court, 1756–70
  Trial and Minute Docket, 1761–90
  Crown Docket, Superior Court, 1767–79
Wilmington
  Minutes, Superior Court, 1760–83

SPECIAL COURT OF OYER AND TERMINER

  1774–75

COUNTY COURTS

Beaufort
  Appearance, Prosecution, and Reference Dockets, 1756–58,
    1756–61
  Appearance, Prosecution, and Reference Dockets, 1756–61,
    1758–61
Bertie
  Minutes, 1724–43
  Miscellaneous Dockets (Crown Dockets), 1725–90
  Miscellaneous Dockets, 1725–90
  Crown Docket, 1762–75
Bute
  Minutes, 1767–76
  Miscellaneous Records
Carteret
  Court Minutes, 1723–47
  Court Dockets, 1731–62
  Court Dockets, 1764–75
  Minutes, August, 1764–December, 1777
  Miscellaneous Court Dockets, 1775–1843
Chowan
  Miscellaneous Court Papers, 1724–1841
  Minutes, April, 1730–October, 1734, January, 1740–January, 1748
  Papers, 1738–41
  Minutes, 1749–55
  Minutes, 1755–61
  Trial Docket, January, 1757–April, 1764
  Execution Dockets, 1757–59, 1765–70

Minute Docket, October, 1761–January, 1766
Dockets, 1763–1806
State Docket, 1774–80
Craven
Minutes, 1730–46
Minutes, 1753–56
Minutes, 1758–61
Minutes, April, 1761–July, 1762
Minutes, January, 1767–March, 1772
Minutes, June, 1777–December, 1778
Cumberland
Minutes, 1755–59, 1759–65
Minutes, January, 1772–January, 1776
Edgecombe
Minutes, 1744–46
Crown Docket, 1755–56
Granville
Minute Docket, 1774–85
Halifax
Crown Docket, 1759–70
Trial Docket, 1766–70
Hyde
Appearance, Crown, Reference, and Prosecution Dockets, 1744–61
Miscellaneous Dockets, 1754–1827
Execution, Reference, and Trial Dockets, 1760–64
Minutes, March, 1761–June, 1764
Execution Docket, 1765
Minutes, 1767–84
Appearance, Crown, Execution, Prosecution, and Reference Dockets, 1767–87
Johnston
Minutes, 1759–67, 1767–77
Mecklenburg
Minutes, 1774–85
New Hanover
Minutes, 1738–68
Minutes, 1738–69
Minutes, 1771–79

Onslow
  Crown Docket, 1745–48
  Crown Docket, 1752
  Crown Docket, 1753–55
  Crown Docket, 1756–59
  Trial Docket, 1759–63
  Crown Docket, 1763–66
  Crown Docket, 1766–74
  Trial Docket, 1774–84
Orange
  Minutes, April, 1737–July, 1753, July, 1754–September, 1777
  Minutes, 1752–66
Pasquotank
  Minutes, April, 1737–July, 1753, July, 1753–September, 1777
  Reference, New Action, Minute Docket, 1753–64, 1755–59, 1763–
    65, 1765–71, 1771–75
Perquimans
  Minutes, 1738–42, 1752–55, 1759–61, 1774
Rowan
  Minutes, 1753–55
  Minutes, 1755–67
  Execution Docket, April, 1761–October, 1766
  Minutes, 1768–72
  Minutes, 1773–86
Tryon
  Minutes, 1769–74, 1774–79
Tyrrell
  Minutes, 1735–61
  Prosecution, Reference, and New Action Dockets, 1756–85
  Minutes, 1761–70

OTHER RECORDS
  Miscellaneous Collections. Slavery Papers, 1747–1850
  Secretary of State. Court Records. Magistrates and Freeholders
    Courts
  Treasurer and Comptroller. Miscellaneous Group, 1738–1909

MANUSCRIPTS

Colonial Office, Ser. 5, Vols. 293, 333. Typewritten transcript in North
Carolina Archives, Raleigh.

Hayes Collection. Southern Historical Collection, University of North
Carolina Library, Chapel Hill.

PUBLISHED SOURCES

Blackstone, Sir William. *Commentaries on the Laws of England.* Vol. IV
of 4 vols. 1765–69; rpr. New York, 1979.

Dalton, Michael. *The Country Justice.* London, 1655.

Davis, James. *The Office and Authority of a Justice of Peace.* Newbern,
1774.

Hawkins, William. *A Treatise of the Pleas of the Crown.* Vol. II of 2 vols.
1724–26; rpr. New York, 1972.

Higginbotham, Don, ed. *The Papers of James Iredell.* Vol. I of 2 vols.
Raleigh, 1976.

Hoffer, Peter C., and William B. Scott, eds. *Criminal Proceedings in
Colonial Virginia: [Records of] Fines, Examination of Criminals,
Trials of Slaves, etc., from March 1710 [1711] to [1754] [Richmond
County, Virginia].* American Legal Records, X. Athens, Ga., 1984.

Jacob, Giles. *Law Dictionary.* London, 1750.

"Journal of Waightstill Avery." *North Carolina University Magazine,* IV
(1855), 242–64.

Lawson, John. *A New Voyage to Carolina.* Edited by Hugh T. Lefler.
Chapel Hill, 1967.

Miranda, Francisco de. *The New Democracy in America.* Translated by
Judson P. Wood. Edited by John S. Ezell. Norman, 1963.

North Carolina Gazette, June 16, 1753, and July 14, 1775.

Parker, Mattie Erma Edwards, William S. Price, Jr., and Robert Cain, eds.
North Carolina Higher-Court Records. 5 vols. Raleigh, 1963–81.

Saunders, William L., Stephen B. Weeks, and Walter Clark, eds. *The
Colonial and State Records of North Carolina.* 30 vols. Raleigh,
Winston, Goldsboro, and Charlotte, 1886–1914.

Schaw, Janet. *Journal of a Lady of Quality.* Edited by Evangeline W.
Andrews and Charles M. Andrews. New Haven, 1923.

Smith, Joseph H., ed. *Colonial Justice in Western Massachusetts,
(1639–1702): The Pynchon Court Record.* Cambridge, Mass., 1961.

Wood, Thomas. *An Institute of the Laws of England.* Vol. IV of 4 vols.
London, 1724.

Woodmason, Charles. *The Carolina Backcountry on the Eve of the Revolution.* Edited by Richard J. Hooker. Chapel Hill, 1953.

SECONDARY SOURCES

BOOKS

Ayers, Edward L. *Vengeance and Justice: Crime and Punishment in the 19th-Century American South.* New York, 1984.

Bellamy, John. *Crime and Public Order in England in the Later Middle Ages.* Toronto, 1973.

Bodenhamer, David J., and James W. Ely, Jr., eds. *Ambivalent Legacy: A Legal History of the South.* Jackson, 1984.

Brewer, John, and John Styles, eds. *An Ungovernable People: The English and Their Law in the Seventeenth and Eighteenth Centuries.* Brunswick, N.J., 1980.

Bryson, William H. *Census of Law Books in Colonial Virginia.* Charlottesville, 1978.

Chapin, Bradley. *Criminal Justice in Colonial America, 1606–1660.* Athens, Ga., 1983.

Cheney, John, Jr., ed. *North Carolina Government 1585–1974.* Raleigh, 1975.

Chumbley, George L. *Colonial Justice in Virginia.* Richmond, 1938.

Cockburn, J. S. *A History of English Assizes, 1558–1714.* Cambridge, England, 1972.

———, ed. *Crime in England 1550–1800.* Princeton, 1977.

Cook, Edward M., Jr. *The Fathers of the Towns: Leadership and Community Structure in Eighteenth-Century New England.* Baltimore, 1976.

Corbitt, David L. *The Formation of the North Carolina Counties, 1663–1943.* Raleigh, 1950.

Crow, Jeffrey J. *The Black Experience in Revolutionary North Carolina.* Raleigh, 1977.

Crow, Jeffrey J., and Flora J. Hatley, eds. *Black Americans in North Carolina and the South.* Chapel Hill, 1984.

Crow, Jeffrey J., and Larry E. Tise, eds. *The Southern Experience in the American Revolution.* Chapel Hill, 1978.

Demos, John. *A Little Commonwealth: Family Life in Plymouth Colony.* New York, 1970.

Ekirch, A. Roger. *"Poor Carolina": Politics and Society in Colonial North Carolina, 1729–1776.* Chapel Hill, 1981.

Erikson, Kai T. *Wayward Puritans: A Study in the Sociology of Deviance.* New York, 1966.

Flaherty, David, ed. *Essays in the History of Early American Law.* Chapel Hill, 1969.

Friedman, Lawrence M. *A History of American Law.* New York, 1973.

Gawalt, Gerard W. *The Promise of Power: The Legal Profession in Massachusetts, 1760–1840.* Westport, Conn., 1979.

Goebel, Julius, Jr., and Thomas R. Naughton. *Law Enforcement in Colonial New York: A Study in Criminal Procedure, 1664–1776.* 1944; rpr. Montclair, N.J., 1970.

Greenberg, Douglas. *Crime and Law Enforcement in the Colony of New York, 1691–1776.* Ithaca, 1974.

Greene, Evarts B., and Virginia D. Harrington. *American Population Before the Federal Census of 1790.* New York, 1932.

Greene, Jack P. *The Quest for Power: The Lower Houses of Assembly in the Southern Royal Colonies, 1689–1776.* Chapel Hill, 1963.

Grimes, J. Bryan. *Abstract of North Carolina Wills.* Raleigh, 1910.

––––––. *North Carolina Wills and Inventories.* Raleigh, 1912.

Hall, David D., John M. Murrin, and Thad W. Tate, eds. *Saints and Revolutionaries: Essays on Early American History.* New York, 1984.

Hamlin, Paul M. *Legal Education in Colonial New York.* 1939; rpr. New York, 1970.

Hamlin, Paul M., and Charles E. Baker, eds. *Supreme Court of Judicature of the Province of New York.* 3 vols. New York, 1959.

Hay, Douglas, *et al. Albion's Fatal Tree: Crime and Society in Eighteenth-Century England.* New York, 1975.

Herrup, Cynthia B. *The Common Peace: Participation and the Criminal Law in Seventeenth-Century England.* Cambridge, England, 1987.

Hewlett, Crocket W. *Attorneys of New Hanover County.* New Hanover, 1976.

Hindus, Michael S. *Prison and Plantation: Crime, Justice, and Authority in Massachusetts and South Carolina, 1767–1878.* Chapel Hill, 1980.

Hoffer, Peter C., and N. E. H. Hull. *Murdering Mothers: Infanticide in England and New England, 1558–1803.* New York, 1981.

Jones, E. Alfred. *American Members of the Inns of Court*. London, 1924.

Jordan, Winthrop. *White Over Black: American Attitudes Toward the Negro, 1550–1812*. Chapel Hill, 1968.

Karraker, Cyrus H. *The Seventeenth-Century Sheriff*. Chapel Hill, 1930.

Koehler, Lyle. *A Search for Power: The "Weaker Sex" in Seventeenth-Century New England*. Urbana, 1980.

Konig, David T. *Law and Society in Puritan Massachusetts: Essex County, 1629–1692*. Chapel Hill, 1979.

Kurtz, Stephen G., and James H. Hutson, eds. *Essays on the American Revolution*. Chapel Hill, 1973.

Lee, Lawrence. *The Lower Cape Fear in Colonial Days*. Chapel Hill, 1965.

Lefler, Hugh T., and William S. Powell. *Colonial North Carolina: A History*. New York, 1973.

McCain, Paul M. *The County Court in North Carolina before 1750*. Historical Papers of the Trinity College Historical Society, No. 31. Durham, 1954.

Main, Jackson Turner. *The Social Structure of Revolutionary America*. Princeton, 1965.

Mays, John B. *Crime and the Social Structure*. London, 1963.

Merrens, Harry R. *Colonial North Carolina in the Eighteenth Century: A Study in Historical Geography*. Chapel Hill, 1964.

Morgan, Edmund S. *The Puritan Family: Religion and Domestic Relations in Seventeenth-Century New England*. New York, 1944.

Osborne, Bertram. *Justices of the Peace 1361–1848*. Dorset, 1960.

Page, Elwin. *Judicial Beginnings in New Hampshire, 1640–1700*. Concord, 1959.

Piers, Maria. *Infanticide*. New York, 1978.

Plucknett, Theodore F. T. *A Concise History of the Common Law*. New York, 1936.

Pollock, Sir Frederick, and Frederic W. Maitland. Vol. II of 2 vols. *The History of English Law*. Cambridge, England, 1898.

Powell, William S., ed. *Dictionary of North Carolina Biography*. Vol. I of 2 vols. Chapel Hill, 1979–.

Powers, Edwin. *Crime and Punishment in Early Massachusetts, 1620–1692: a documentary history*. Boston, 1966.

Rankin, Hugh F. *Criminal Trial Proceedings in the General Court of Colonial Virginia*. Charlottesville, 1965.

Raper, Charles L. *North Carolina: A Study in English Colonial Government*. 1904; rpr. Spartanburg, 1973.

Roeber, A. G. *Faithful Magistrates and Republican Lawyers: Creators of Virginia Legal Culture, 1680–1810*. Chapel Hill, 1981.

Rumple, Rev. Jethro. *A History of Rowan County, North Carolina*. Salisbury, 1881.

Samaha, Joel. *Law and Order in Historical Perspective: The Case of Elizabethan Essex*. New York, 1974.

Scott, Arthur P. *Criminal Law in Colonial Virginia*. Chicago, 1930.

Semmes, Raphael. *Crime and Punishment in Early Maryland*. Baltimore, 1938.

Simon, Rita J. *Women and Crime*. Lexington, Mass., 1975.

Sirmans, M. Eugene. *Colonial South Carolina: A Political History, 1663–1763*. Chapel Hill, 1966.

Smith, Abbot E. *Colonists in Bondage: White Servitude and Convict Labor in America, 1607–1776*. New York, 1947.

Spruill, Julia Cherry. *Women's Life and Work in the Southern Colonies*. 1938; rpr. New York, 1972.

Sydnor, Charles S. *American Revolutionaries in the Making*. 1952; rpr. New York, 1965.

Thompson, E. P. *Whigs and Hunters: The Origin of the Black Act*. New York, 1975.

Thompson, Roger. *Women in Stuart England and America*. London, 1974.

Weiss, Harry B., and Grace M. Weiss. *An Introduction to Crime and Punishment in Colonial New Jersey*. Trenton, 1960.

Wheeler, John H. *Reminiscences and Memoirs of North Carolina*. Columbus, Ohio, 1884.

Wrigley, E. A., ed. *Nineteenth Century Society: Essays in the use of quantitative methods for the study of social data*. Cambridge, England, 1972.

Young, Alfred F., ed. *The American Revolution: Explorations in the History of American Radicalism*. De Kalb, Ill., 1976.

Younger, Richard D. *The People's Panel: The Grand Jury in the United States, 1634–1941*. Providence, 1963.

Zuckerman, Michael. *Peaceable Kingdoms: New England Towns in the Eighteenth Century*. New York, 1970.

ARTICLES AND ESSAYS

Alderman, Ernest H. "The North Carolina Bar." In *James Sprunt Historical Publications,* edited by J. G. de Roulhac Hamilton and Henry M. Wagstaff. Vol. XIII. Durham, 1913.

Bassett, John S. "The Regulators of North Carolina, 1765–1771." American Historical Association, *Annual Report for the Year 1894.* Washington, D.C., 1895, pp. 141–212.

Baumgartner, M. P. "Law and Social Status in Colonial New Haven, 1639–1665." *Research in Law and Sociology,* I (1978), 153–74.

Beattie, J. M. "The Criminality of Women in Eighteenth-Century England." *Journal of Social History,* VIII (1975), 80–116.

Billings, Warren M. "English Legal Literature as a Source of Law and Legal Practice for Seventeenth-Century Virginia." *Virginia Magazine of History and Biography,* LXXXVII (1979), 403–16.

Boyd, Julian P. "The Sheriff in Colonial North Carolina." *North Carolina Historical Review,* V (1928), 151–81.

Canady, Hoyt P. "Legal Education in Colonial South Carolina." In *South Carolina Legal History,* edited by Herbert A. Johnson. Spartanburg, 1980.

Conley, John A. "Criminal Justice History as a Field of Research: A Review of the Literature, 1960–1975." *Journal of Criminal Justice,* V (1977), 13–28.

Corbitt, David L. "Judicial Districts of North Carolina, 1746–1934." *North Carolina Historical Review,* XII (1935), 45–61.

Eaton, Clement. "A Mirror of the Southern Colonial Lawyer." *William and Mary Quarterly,* 3rd ser., VIII (1951), 520–34.

Ekirch, A. Roger. "North Carolina Regulators on Liberty and Corruption." *Perspectives in American History,* XI (1977–78), 199–256.

Elliot, Robert N., Jr. "James Davis and the Beginning of the Newspaper in North Carolina." *North Carolina Historical Review,* XLII (1965), 1–20.

Faber, Eli. "Puritan Criminals: The Economic, Social, and Intellectual Background to Crime in Seventeenth-Century Massachusetts." *Perspectives in American History,* XI (1977–78), 81–144.

Flaherty, David. "Law and the Enforcement of Morals in Early America." In *American Law and the Constitutional Order,* edited by Lawrence Friedman and Harry Scheiber. Cambridge, Mass., 1978.

Gallman, James M. "Determinants of Age at Marriage in Colonial

Perquimans County, North Carolina." *William and Mary Quarterly,* 3rd ser., XXXIX (1982), 176–91.

Gipson, Lawrence H. "Crime and Its Punishment in Provincial Pennsylvania." *Lehigh University Publications,* IX (1935), 1–14.

Graff, Harvey J. "Crime and Punishment in the Nineteenth Century: A New Look at the Criminal." *Journal of Interdisciplinary History,* VII (1977), 477–91.

Greenberg, Douglas. "The Effectiveness of Law Enforcement in Eighteenth-Century New York." *American Journal of Legal History,* XIX (1975), 173–207.

———. "Crime, Law Enforcement, and Social Control in Colonial America." *American Journal of Legal History,* XXVI (1982), 293–325.

Greene, Jack P. "Legislative Turnover in British America, 1696–1775: A Quantitative Analysis." *William and Mary Quarterly,* 3rd ser., XXXVIII (1981), 442–63.

Hamilton, J. G. de Roulhac. "Southern Members of the Inns of Court." *North Carolina Historical Review,* X (1933), 273–86.

Hemphill, C. Dallett. "Women in Court: Sex-Role Differentiation in Salem, Massachusetts, 1636–1683." *William and Mary Quarterly,* 3rd ser., XXXIX (1982), 164–75.

Herrup, Cynthia B. "New Shoes and Mutton Pies: Investigative Responses to Theft in Seventeenth-Century East Sussex." *Historical Journal,* XXVII (1984), 811–30.

———. "Law and Morality in Seventeenth-Century England." *Past and Present,* CVI (1985), 102–23.

Higginbotham, Don, and William S. Price, Jr. "Was It Murder for a White Man to Kill a Slave? Chief Justice Martin Howard Condemns the Peculiar Institution in North Carolina." *William and Mary Quarterly,* 3rd ser., XXXVI (1979), 593–601.

Hindus, Michael S. "The Social Context of Crime in Massachusetts and South Carolina, 1760–1783: Theoretical and Quantitative Perspectives." Newberry Papers in Family and Community History, 1975.

Hindus, Michael S., and Jones, Douglas Lamar. "Quantitative Methods or *Quantum Meruit?* Tactics for Early American Legal History." *Historical Methods,* XIII (1980), 63–74.

Kammen, Michael G. "Colonial Court Records and American History." *American Historical Review,* LXX (1965), 732–39.

Kay, Marvin L. Michael, and Lorin Lee Cary. " 'The Planters Suffer

Little or Nothing': North Carolina Compensations for Executed Slaves, 1748–1772." *Science and Society,* XL (1976), 288–306.

———, and Lorin Lee Cary. " 'They are Indeed the Constant Plague of Their Tyrants': Slave Defence of a Moral Economy in Colonial North Carolina, 1748–1772." *Slavery and Abolition,* VI (1985), 37–56.

———, and Lorin Lee Cary. "Slave Runaways in Colonial North Carolina, 1748–1775." *North Carolina Historical Review,* LXIII (1986), 1–39.

King, Walter J. "Punishment for Bastardy in Early Seventeenth-Century England." *Albion,* X (1978), 130–51.

Land, Aubrey C. "Economic Base and Social Structure: The Northern Chesapeake in the Eighteenth Century." *Journal of Economic History,* XXV (1965), 639–54.

Langbein, John H. "Shaping the Eighteenth-Century Criminal Trial: A View from the Ryder Sources." *University of Chicago Law Review,* L (1983), 1–135.

McCain, Paul M. "Magistrates Courts in Early North Carolina." *North Carolina Historical Review,* XLVIII (1971), 23–30.

Moller, Herbert. "Sex Composition and Correlated Culture Patterns of Colonial America." *William and Mary Quarterly,* 3rd ser., II (1945), 112–53.

Nelson, William E. "Emerging Notions of Modern Criminal Law in the Revolutionary Era." *New York University Law Review,* XLII (1967), 450–66.

Preyer, Kathryn. "Penal Measures in the American Colonies: An Overview." *American Journal of Legal History,* XXVI (1982), 326–53.

Price, William S., Jr. " 'Men of Good Estates': Wealth Among North Carolina's Royal Councillors." *North Carolina Historical Review,* XLIX (1972), 72–82.

———. "A Strange Incident in George Burrington's Royal Governorship." *North Carolina Historical Review,* LI (1974), 149–58.

Rowe, G. S. "Women's Crime and Criminal Administration in Pennsylvania, 1763–1790." *Pennsylvania Magazine of History and Biography,* CIX (1985), 335–68.

Smith, Daniel Scott. "The Demographic History of Colonial New England." *Journal of Economic History,* XXXII (1972), 165–83.

Smith, Daniel Scott, and Michael S. Hindus. "Premarital Pregnancy in America, 1640–1971: An Overview and Interpretation." *Journal of Interdisciplinary History,* V (1975), 537–70.

Spindel, Donna J. "Law and Disorder: The North Carolina Stamp Act Crisis." *North Carolina Historical Review,* LVII (1980), 1–16.

———. "The Administration of Justice in North Carolina, 1720–1740." *American Journal of Legal History,* XXV (1981), 141–62.

Spindel, Donna J., and Stuart W. Thomas, Jr. "Crime and Society in North Carolina, 1663–1740." *Journal of Southern History,* XLIX (1983), 223–44.

Thornton, Mary Lindsay. "Public Printing in North Carolina, 1749–1815." *North Carolina Historical Review,* XXI (1944), 181–202.

Tilly, Louise, Joan W. Scott, and Miriam Cohen. "Women's Work and European Fertility Patterns." In *The American Family in Social-Historical Perspective,* edited by Michael Gordon. New York, 1978.

Towne, Susan C. "The Historical Origins of Bench Trial for Serious Crime." *American Journal of Legal History,* XXVI (1982), 123–59.

Watson, Alan D. "Sheriffs in Colonial North Carolina." *North Carolina Historical Review,* LIII (1976), 385–98.

———. "Impulse Toward Independence: Resistance and Rebellion Among North Carolina Slaves, 1750–1775." *Journal of Negro History,* LXIII (1978), 317–28.

———. "Women in Colonial North Carolina." *North Carolina Historical Review,* LVIII (1981), 1–22.

Watson, Helen R. "The Books They Left: Some 'Liberies' in Edgecombe County, 1733–1783." *North Carolina Historical Review,* XLVIII (1971), 245–57.

Weeks, Stephen B. "Libraries and Literature in North Carolina in the Eighteenth Century." American Historical Association, *Annual Report for the Year 1895.* Washington, D.C., 1896.

Wells, Robert V. "Illegitimacy and Bridal Pregnancy in Colonial America." In *Bastardy and its Comparative History,* edited by Peter Laslett, Karla Osterveen, and Richard M. Smith. Cambridge, Mass., 1980.

Wiener, Carol Z. "Sex-Roles and Crime in Late Elizabethan Hertfordshire." *Journal of Social History,* VIII (1975), 38–60.

———. "Is a Spinster an Unmarried Woman?" *American Journal of Legal History,* XX (1976), 27–31.

Whittenburg, James P. "Planters, Merchants, and Lawyers: Social Change and the Origins of the North Carolina Regulation." *William and Mary Quarterly,* 3rd ser., XXXIV (1977), 215–38.

Yackel, Peter G. "Benefit of Clergy in Colonial Maryland." *Maryland Historical Magazine,* LXIX (1974), 383–97.

Zanger, Jules. "Crime and Punishment in Early Massachusetts." *William and Mary Quarterly,* 3rd ser., XXII (1955), 471–77.

DISSERTATIONS AND PAPERS

Freedman, Estelle Brenda. "Their Sisters' Keepers: The Origins of Female Corrections in America." Ph.D. dissertation, Columbia University, 1976.

Hull, N. E. H. "Female Felons: Women and Serious Crime in the Superior Court of Massachusetts, 1673–1774." Ph.D. dissertation, Columbia University, 1981.

Simon, Rita J., and Navin Sharma. "The Female Defendant in Washington, D.C., 1974–1975." Institute for Law and Social Research. Washington, D.C., 1978.

Stevenson, George, and Ruby D. Arnold. *North Carolina Courts of Law and Equity Prior to 1868.* Archives Information Circular, No. 9. Raleigh, 1977.

INDEX

Adultery: legislation on, 50; defined, 105; prosecutions, 118, 119, 131, 133; punishment, 118, 119, 131, 133; mentioned, 63. *See also* Disposition of cases; Prosecution patterns

Affray: defined, 52–53. *See also* Disposition of cases; Prosecution patterns

Albemarle region: creation of, 2; privileged position, 3, 4, 7; economy, 6; disorder in, 7, 10; rivalry with Cape Fear region, 10; contempt in, 64

Allen, Eleazer, 33

Allen family, 3, 31

American Revolution, 15–16

Animal stealing: prosecutions, 39, 52, 62, 92*n*, 122; defined, 47; incidence of, 61–62, 66; legislation on, 61–62, 122; and Indians, 74; punishment, 122, 125, 131, 135–36. *See also* Disposition of cases; Prosecution patterns

Anson County, 13, 53

Appeals, 41

Arson: prosecutions, 66, 75, 113; punishment, 125; mentioned, 53

Artisan: defined, 76. *See also* Prosecution patterns

Ashe, Samuel, 33

Ashe family, 3

Assault: prosecutions, 27, 49, 50, 51, 52, 74–75, 119–20, 135; defined, 49;

incidence of, 55, 59–60, 68; guilty pleas, 94; punishment, 119, 120, 131, 135, 137; mentioned, 53. *See also* Disposition of cases; Prosecution patterns; Punishment

Assembly: clashes with governor, 9–10, 12, 15; meets at Wilmington, 10; corruption of, 12, 14; resists Martin's reforms, 15; requires law books in courts, 28. *See also* Privy Council

Assize courts. *See* Circuit courts

Associate justice: of General Court, 20; described, 31; training, 31–32; plural office-holding, 32

Attorneys: reputation, 32–33; training 33–34; libraries of, 34; defense role, 38–39. *See also* Criminal procedure

Avery, Waightstill, 34, 39

Bail, 37

Barker, Thomas, 28*n*, 33, 38

Bastardy: legislation on, 50; incidence of, 62–63, 85; prosecutions, 85, 129, 131; punishment, 118, 129, 131; mentioned, 37. *See also* Disposition of cases; Prosecution patterns

Bath: circuit court created, 22

Bath County: established, 2–3; and Cary Rebellion, 7

Beaufort County: county court prosecutions, 113, 118*n*

Benefit of clergy: form of pardon, 41;